Teach Yourself VISUALLY™
Circular Knitting

by Melissa Morgan-Oakes

WILEY

Wiley Publishing, Inc.

Teach Yourself VISUALLY™ *Circular Knitting*

Copyright © 2011 by Melissa Morgan-Oakes. All rights reserved.

Published by Wiley Publishing, Inc., Hoboken, New Jersey

For general information on our other products and services or to obtain technical support please contact our Customer Care Department within the U.S. at (877) 762-2974, outside the U.S. at (317) 572-3993 or fax (317) 572-4002.

Wiley also publishes its books in a variety of electronic formats. Some content that appears in print may not be available in electronic books. For more information about Wiley products, please visit our web site at www.wiley.com.

Library of Congress Control Number: 2011924893

ISBN: 978-0-470-87426-4
eISBN: 978-1-118-07588-3, 9781118167090 & 9781118167083

Printed in the United States of America

10 9 8 7 6 5 4 3 2

Book production by Wiley Publishing, Inc. Composition Services

Updates to this book are available on the Downloads tab at this site: http://www.wiley.com/WileyCDA/WileyTitle/productCd-0470874260.html. If a Downloads tab does not appear at this link, there are no updates at this time.

Praise for the Teach Yourself VISUALLY Series

I just had to let you and your company know how great I think your books are. I just purchased my third Visual book (my first two are dog-eared now!) and, once again, your product has surpassed my expectations. The expertise, thought, and effort that go into each book are obvious, and I sincerely appreciate your efforts. Keep up the wonderful work!

—*Tracey Moore (Memphis, TN)*

I have several books from the Visual series and have always found them to be valuable resources.

—*Stephen P. Miller (Ballston Spa, NY)*

Thank you for the wonderful books you produce. It wasn't until I was an adult that I discovered how I learn—visually. Although a few publishers out there claim to present the material visually, nothing compares to Visual books. I love the simple layout. Everything is easy to follow. And I understand the material! You really know the way I think and learn. Thanks so much!

—*Stacey Han (Avondale, AZ)*

Like a lot of other people, I understand things best when I see them visually. Your books really make learning easy and life more fun.

—*John T. Frey (Cadillac, MI)*

I am an avid fan of your Visual books. If I need to learn anything, I just buy one of your books and learn the topic in no time. Wonders! I have even trained my friends to give me Visual books as gifts.

—*Illona Bergstrom (Aventura, FL)*

I write to extend my thanks and appreciation for your books. They are clear, easy to follow, and straight to the point. Keep up the good work! I bought several of your books and they are just right! No regrets! I will always buy your books because they are the best.

—*Seward Kollie (Dakar, Senegal)*

Credits

Acquisitions Editor
Pam Mourouzis

Project Editor
Suzanne Snyder

Copy Editor
Marylouise Wiack

Technical Editor
Tamara Stone-Snyder

Editorial Manager
Christina Stambaugh

Vice President and Publisher
Cindy Kitchel

Vice President and Executive Publisher
Kathy Nebenhaus

Interior Design
Elizabeth Brooks
Kathie Rickard

Photography
Matt Bowen

Special Thanks...

I am very grateful for the generous support and contributions of the companies who gave their products for use in this book

- Berroco
- Blue Moon Fiber Arts
- Buffalo Gold
- Foxfire Fiber
- Lorna's Laces
- Schaefer Yarn Company
- Spirit Trail Fiberworks
- Valley Yarns

About the Author

Melissa Morgan-Oakes has often been told by her mother that she has "a head just full of useless information," and hopes that comes through on the following pages. One person's useless is another person's necessary! Author of the bestselling *2-at-a-Time Socks* and *Toe-Up 2-at-a-Time Socks*, and a nationally respected knitting instructor and designer, Melissa brings the unique skill and energy of a self-taught knitter to all of her endeavors. She lives, works and maintains a lifestyle blog (www.melissa-knits.blogspot.com) from her small farm in Western Massachusetts where she lives with her husband, pets, a hundred-odd chickens and a half a million or so honey bees.

Acknowledgments

This book is dually dedicated to my father Dan Morgan and my husband Gene Oakes who continue to be my biggest inspiration and strongest support whether I am writing knitting books or chasing chickens, among many other things.

Special thanks to Cindy Kitchel, Pam Mourouzis, and Suzanne Snyder at Wiley Publishing, my wonderful technical editor Tamara Stone-Snyder, and "Agent Linda" Roghaar of Linda Roghaar Literary Agency, without all of whom this project would not have seen the light of day.

To my sample knitters Mary-Alice Baker, Mary Kubasek-Haber, Dena Childs, Sara Delaney, Kristen Gonsalves, and Katy Wight; my undying gratitude for the handiwork you put in on this project.

To Clara Parkes, Kathy Elkins, Mary, Kristen, and anyone else I tormented with tantrums and whines; thank you so much for listening to, encouraging, commiserating with, and cajoling me when the moment required it.

Table of Contents

CHAPTER 3 Special Techniques for Circular Knitting

CHAPTER 4 Starter Projects

Table of Contents

CHAPTER 5 Planning a Project

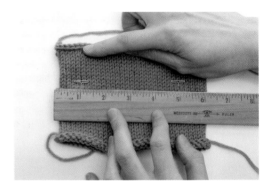

CHAPTER 6 Simple Projects

CHAPTER 7   Intermediate Projects

CHAPTER 8   Advanced Projects

Table of Contents

CHAPTER 9 Steeked Projects

CHAPTER 10 Stitch Gallery

CHAPTER 1

Introduction to Circular Knitting

Whether you call it circular knitting or knitting in the round, it means the same thing: knitting items as tubes (or, more correctly, spirals) instead of knitting flat pieces back-and-forth. The information in this book will help you discover new ways to use your knitting tools to increase efficiency in the construction and finishing of your projects. I hope that you will learn to love working in the round and will bring these techniques into all aspects of your knitting life.

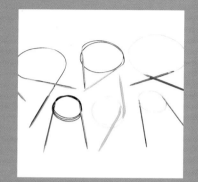

About Circular Knitting

Circular knitting differs from flat knitting in several ways. In flat knitting, you typically use single-pointed needles and work back and forth in rows. When you reach the end of a row, you turn your project over and work back. However, in circular knitting, you use different kinds of needles that allow you to keep knitting in one direction around the outside of your project (see the "Needles for Circular Knitting" section later in this chapter). The knitting develops in a spiral, and you normally do not turn the work unless you are performing special shaping techniques. Circular knitting is therefore counted in *rounds* instead of *rows*.

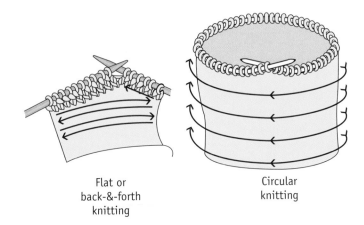

Flat or
back-&-forth
knitting

Circular
knitting

Because the right side of your work is always facing you, you work most stitch patterns differently in the round than when working flat. For instance, when working flat, you create stockinette stitch by knitting each right-side row and purling each wrong-side row, as shown here. However, in circular knitting *all rounds* are right-side rounds, so you must knit every round to create a stockinette fabric. You create garter stitch in flat knitting by knitting a right-side row and then knitting a wrong-side row. However, when working garter stitch in the round, you must knit one round and then purl the next. This may sound complicated now, but once you try circular knitting, you will quickly get the idea.

A lot of things can be knit in the round; in fact, most things can be. Any item that is made up of a tube of some sort lends itself well to being worked in the round. This includes garments such as hats, socks, mittens, and skirts as well as household items and accessories such as purses, tote bags, pillow covers, wine bottle covers, yoga mat bags, and a variety of cozies for digital devices.

With more complicated projects that consist of many connected tubes, such as pullovers or gloves, you can work in the round with additional shaping. You can even work projects such as cardigans, scarves, and shawls in the round and later cut them apart (a process called *steeking;* see Chapter 9 for details).

The Pros and Cons of Knitting in the Round

There are many advantages to circular knitting, which is why I choose to knit my projects in the round whenever I can. However, as with everything in life, there are certain aspects of circular knitting that some people see as drawbacks. I strongly believe that the benefits of circular knitting outweigh any small challenges, especially since those challenges are so easy to overcome. I think you will agree with me.

Advantages of Knitting in the Round

LESS PURLING

Some knitters dislike purling. Depending on your style of knitting, which is a topic that could fill a whole other book, purling can be a little slower than knitting. If you often work in stockinette and dislike purling, then you will love circular knitting. Since you work in a spiral around the outside of the piece, when working in stockinette you can just knit, knit, and knit some more. It can be quite relaxing to knit in the round on a stockinette project!

LESS SEAMING

Another benefit of working in the round is that you don't have to do as much seaming, and in some instances no seaming at all. Take socks or mittens, for example: if you work them as tubes with some shaping here and there for a thumb or a heel, then your seaming will be nonexistent. Many types of garments are really much more comfortable when constructed without seams, such as socks, mittens, hats, and, in my opinion, sweaters. Seams can be stiff and bulky, making garments uncomfortable in places where there is a lot of friction, like underarms or cuffs.

In circular knitting, if you knit the sleeves of a sweater in the round, you don't need to seam them up when you are done. If you knit the body of the sweater in the round, you can easily attach the sleeves while you are knitting the sweater, instead of having to sew them in afterward. You will see examples of attaching sleeves to a garment in progress in Chapter 8, but the idea is that by knitting pieces as tubes, you can eliminate or lessen the need for seaming, saving yourself a lot of time and creating a garment that is more comfortable to wear.

RIGHT SIDE ALWAYS FACING YOU

In most cases, circular knitting means that the "right" or public side of the work is facing you. When working with stranded colorwork, circular knitting can make it easier to track your pattern. Working with the design facing you, such as with a cable panel like the one shown here, helps you keep the different colors where they are supposed to be. The same is true of any patterned project, such as lace, cables, or knit-and-purl patterns. With the right side always facing you, the path of a charted pattern is simpler to follow, which means fewer mistakes.

PORTABILITY

Many knitters find projects worked in the round, especially those knit on circular needles, to be more portable than those knit on straight needles. The flexible cable helps a project fit readily into your knitting bag. When working with circular needles, you can slide the stitches to the center of the cable, where they are less likely to slide off the needle tips. For added protection, you can use a simple rubber band to hold the two needle ends together, although in most cases this extra step isn't needed.

EASE IN CHECKING FIT

One of the nicest benefits of knitting in the round is that you can try on garments as you go, making adjustments as needed. For instance, when knitting a sleeve in the round, it's easy to slip it on and check the length. However, if you worked flat, you would have to pin or temporarily seam the sleeve together before trying it on. Working a hat in the round allows you to try it on to check the fit: both the circumference of the brim and the depth of the hat. Instead of measuring and wondering when to stop, trying on the item ensures that you get a better fit.

MORE CONSISTENT GAUGE

Some people knit and purl at different tensions or use a bit more yarn when they purl. As a result, their gauge can be inconsistent when working an item in flat, back-and-forth knitting. This is sometimes referred to as *rowing out*. When working in stockinette stitch, this appears as a slightly shorter row of knit stitches alternating with a slightly elongated row of stitches. Knitting in the round corrects this problem by allowing you to always be working on the outside of the piece.

COMFORT AND ERGONOMICS

Knitting a heavy project on single-pointed needles can place a lot of strain on your hands, wrists, and elbows as the weight of the project hangs from the distant ends of your straight needles. However, this is less of a problem with circular knitting because the project hangs from the cable, so the weight is more centralized. The same holds true for objects knit on double-pointed needles. As you knit, the weight of the project falls from the needles straight down into your lap.

KNITTING TWO-AT-A-TIME

Working with the technique commonly called "magic loop" (see Chapter 2), you can knit more than one item at a time. My books *2-at-a-Time Socks* and *Toe-Up 2-at-a-Time Socks* both explain this technique in detail. You can expand the concept from socks to anything that you knit as a tube and that you need two of—sleeves, mittens, baby booties, and so on. When finished, items that you construct in this way are exactly the same size. Knitting things at the same time also eliminates the need to go back and repeat the work you've just done.

LESS ROW COUNTING

When working a sweater flat, you must count the rows on the front and back or carefully measure and match their lengths to ensure that the pieces will match up when you seam them. However, with circular knitting, you can knit the body of a sweater in one piece, so there's no need to worry about working the same number of rows for the front and back.

Disadvantages of Knitting in the Round

Even though "no seams" is one of the best parts of circular knitting, it can also cause a few difficulties. Fortunately, you can easily overcome these challenges.

NO SEAMS IN WHICH TO HIDE ENDS

In flat knitting, seams give you a place to hide the ends of yarn when changing colors or attaching a new ball of yarn. Since there are no seams in circular knitting, there is also "no place to hide." This means you must be a little tidier when weaving in your ends or use an alternative method such as spit-splicing or a Russian join to eliminate ends altogether (see Chapter 3 for details about joining new yarn in circular knitting). However, I see this as a good thing; the seams in flat knitting can quickly become overloaded with yarn ends, which can create bulk.

NO SIDE SEAMS ON SWEATERS

Some people object to knitting sweaters in the round because they actually *want* seams. They feel that side seams add definition and stability to a sweater, or they just prefer the look of a sweater with a side seam. It is true that seams can prevent sagging in some very stretchy stitch patterns. However, if you want to make the appearance of a seam or desire added stability in a particular project, there are ways to do that while still knitting in the round. You can create a false seam in the location where a seam would naturally fall in a garment knit back and forth (see Chapter 3). A false seam gives both the appearance and the stability of a seam.

JOGS ON HORIZONTAL STRIPES

In flat knitting, you work horizontal stripes and color-work patterns back and forth in rows. When you seam the piece later, you can match up these stripes nearly exactly on each side to make each stripe appear to be a perfect circle. It's a fussy business, but you can do it.

When you work horizontal stripes or colorwork patterns in the round, you are really working them as spirals. This means that the last stitch you knit at the end of a round will appear raised above the first stitch of that round. This creates a little stairstep called a "color jog" whenever you change colors. Fortunately, there are techniques to compensate for this (see Chapter 3). A *jogless jog* eliminates both the visible color change and the need for fussy post-knitting color matching in seams.

LARGE PROJECTS CAN BECOME UNWIELDY

Knitting a large project, such as a pullover, in the round can get heavy. Some people therefore prefer to knit large items like this in pieces, which lessens the weight and increases the portability. However, remember that if you knit a sweater in the round, there is no, or nearly no, seaming when you are done. And this extra bulk falls into your lap rather than putting additional strain on your hands, wrists, and elbows. I'm very happy to work with a few extra ounces of yarn in my lap in exchange for all the benefits that circular knitting brings.

You use two types of needles in circular knitting: double-pointed and circular. Although some types of projects are more easily worked using certain needles, the needle you choose is largely a matter of personal preference. The information below can help you make informed decisions when buying needles for circular knitting.

Double-Pointed Needles

Double-pointed needles, commonly called *dpns*, are straight needles that are pointed on both ends. They are good for working on projects with a small circumference, such as mittens, socks, or the fingers of gloves. You divide your stitches among the needles (sold in sets of four or five) and work in a continuous spiral from one needle to the next, forming a tube of knitted fabric.

NOTE: I prefer sets of five because I am notorious for losing needles. The fifth needle is like an insurance plan—if I lose one, I still have the other four to work with.

SIZES

Double-pointed needles are available in all standard needle sizes ranging from tiny 8/0 (pronounced "eight-ought") to very large US 36 (20mm).

Sold in lengths ranging from 4 to 16 inches, dpns are most commonly found in 5- to 8-inch lengths. The shortest needles can be uncomfortable to hold and are best suited to working the fingers of gloves and other items with a small circumference. You can use long dpns for working sweaters or other large projects, but they can be unwieldy.

MATERIALS

Like straight needles, double-pointed needles are available in a wide range of materials to suit individual tastes and needs. You can find them made of plastic, aluminum, steel, bamboo, and various types of wood. The very smallest sizes are available only in steel; in other materials they would likely break.

For beginners, I highly recommend bamboo or unpolished wooden needles. The slight texture on the surface of these needles helps keep the stitches from accidentally slipping off the ends. Plastic dpns also have some surface friction for holding your stitches and are lightweight. If you're looking for speed, then metal needles are the way to go. Their slick, polished surface lets the stitches move quickly on the needles. However, metal dpns can be relatively heavy, causing them to occasionally slip from your work, especially if you are a loose knitter.

DOUBLE-POINTED NEEDLE RECOMMENDATIONS

For beginning circular knitters who are working on mittens, socks, hats, and similar items, I recommend a five-needle set of wooden or bamboo needles. Good choices include Clover bamboo needles and Brittany birch needles. To treat yourself, try a set of DyakCraft's Darn Pretty needles, which are made from a laminated composite wood product and are available in a wide range of colors, or Blue Sky Alpacas' reclaimed Dalbergia Rosewood needles. As you gain skill and confidence with knitting in the round, consider experimenting with other needles.

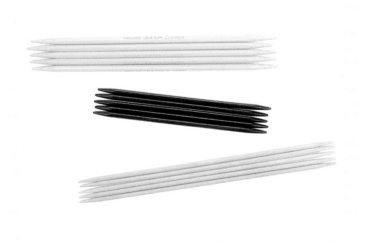

Circular Needles

A circular needle consists of two needle tips connected by a thin cable. You typically use circulars to knit projects that have a circumference of 18 or more inches. However, you can use them in creative ways to knit smaller circumferences. The length of the circular you need will depend on which method of circular knitting you are using, as well as the circumference of your intended project. I will explain this further in Chapter 2.

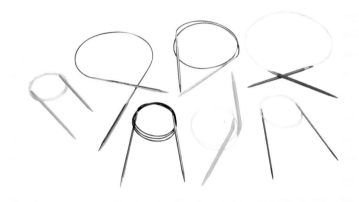

SIZES

As with double-pointed needles, circular needles are available in all standard sizes. However, they are not easy to find in sizes smaller than US 0 or larger than US 19. Circular needles come in many lengths, ranging from 9 to 60 inches. This measurement includes the length of the needles, not just the length of the cable.

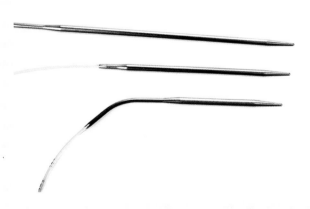

The length of the needle tip varies with the length of the entire circular needle: a 16-inch circular typically has a tip of about $3\frac{1}{2}$ inches, while a 40-inch circular typically has a tip of about 5 inches. Some people prefer to work with long circular needles because there is more needle tip to hold.

MATERIALS

The tips of circular needles can be made from a variety of materials, including wood, bamboo, metal, plastic, and even glass. The cable connecting the tips is commonly made of plastic, nylon, or silicone. Some cables are very flexible, while others maintain some stiffness, making them inappropriate for some methods of circular knitting.

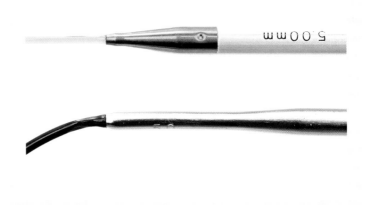

The point where the needle and cable meet is referred to as the *join*. A smooth join is important in a circular needle, because it means your stitches won't snag as you slide them from the cable onto the needles, making for a more pleasant knitting experience.

Metal and polished wood needles are slick and smooth, which means that stitches slide faster along the needle. This is especially true of needles with a nickel plating, such as Addi Turbos. Bamboo, plastic, and unpolished wood needles have more texture and drag to help your stitches stay in place. These can be a better choice for beginning knitters or when working complex lace projects. Once you have built up your confidence with a slightly textured needle, you can build your speed with super-slick ones.

TIP

The shortest circular needles (9 inches) have a needle tip that is only 2 inches long. Most people find these needles uncomfortable since there is very little to hold onto. They require you to grasp the needle with just a few fingers, which can lead to hand cramping. I find it much easier to use double-pointed needles or other methods to work such small circumferences (see Chapter 2). The only way to know what works best for you is to experiment with many needle types.

The tips of circular needles range from blunt to pointy. Pointy tips are great for working cables and lace, as they more easily penetrate tight stitch configurations. However, they are more likely to split and snag your yarn. For that reason, some people prefer blunter tips, especially when working plain stockinette or simple stitch patterns.

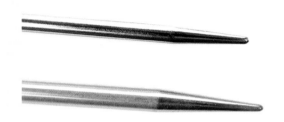

VERSATILITY

Circular needles are very versatile, making them great multipurpose tools. You can use them to work items in the round or flat. To use them for flat knitting, you cast on the stitches required for the intended project and, instead of joining the work (as shown in Chapter 2), you simply turn the work around as if you were using straight needles and work back across the same row. This ability to work with circular needles for back-and-forth projects makes them particularly useful for large, flat items such as afghans or shawls.

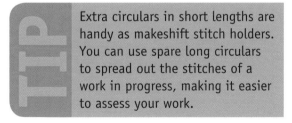

TIP

Extra circulars in short lengths are handy as makeshift stitch holders. You can use spare long circulars to spread out the stitches of a work in progress, making it easier to assess your work.

CIRCULAR NEEDLE RECOMMENDATIONS

Skacel Addi circulars are my favorite needles. Although they cost more, their quality is well worth the investment. The join on Addi circular needles is barely noticeable, and they have a pliable cable. They come in three types: Addi Natura, Addi Turbo, and Addi Lace. Addi Natura needles are made of bamboo with a moderately blunt needle tip and are excellent beginner needles. Addi Turbos are made of nickel-plated brass and are very smooth and fast. They are a great choice for knitters who have experience with circular knitting and are looking to increase their speed. Addi Lace needles are made of polished brass and have a pointy tip that is perfect for working lace or cable projects.

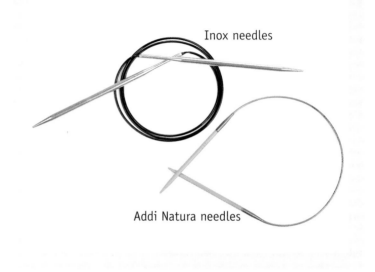

Inox needles

Addi Natura needles

Inox makes two types of circular needles: Inox and Inox Express. Both are affordable and available in yarn shops and through online retailers. The former have gray-coated aluminum needle tips with a clear plastic cable. The coating on the needle creates some friction, making it a great option if you are learning to work in the round. However, the cable is not very flexible. Inox Express circulars have nickel-plated needle tips with a flexible black cable and a smooth join. These needles are among my favorites for their speed and affordability.

Clover Takumi bamboo circular needles are affordably priced and are available in many retail locations. Because they are made of bamboo, they are excellent needles for a beginning circular knitter. However, the join on these circulars can sometimes catch your work.

Many other needles are on the market—so many that I could probably devote an entire chapter to the topic. Of note, **Signature Needle Arts'** precision-made metal needles and **DyakCraft's** colorful, hand-crafted wooden needles qualify as luxury tools; they are a delight to hold in your hands and a joy to knit with. These needles make a wonderful gift that you can give to yourself.

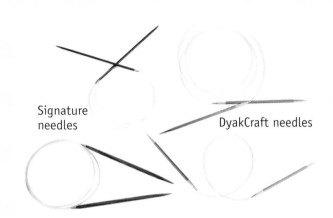

Signature
needles

DyakCraft needles

Crystal Palace and **KA** both produce high-quality bamboo circulars with pliable cables.

HiyaHiya makes affordable metal circulars that are great if you are on a budget.

Kollage makes circulars with square needle tips, which some people find to be more comfortable to hold than traditional needle tips, especially in the larger sizes.

TIP

Experimenting with different types of needles is the best way to determine what works best for you. This doesn't need to be a huge up-front investment. Buy one set at a time and try them for a while before adding another set in a different size and length. Over time, you will accumulate a variety of needles that are suitable for different situations; you will also discover which are your favorites and learn what's best for any given project.

Interchangeable Circular Needle Sets

Circular needles also come in interchangeable sets that enable you to "build your own needle" out of the included needle tips and cables. These sets are available in a variety of materials and feature different methods of connecting the cables to the needles: some turn and click, some push and click, and some screw on and are tightened with a tool.

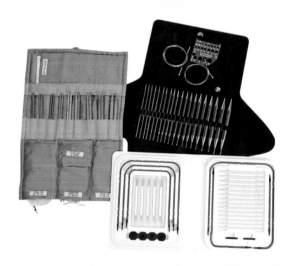

Most sets contain multiple cables of various lengths with pairs of needle tips in sizes from US 4 to 11. Interchangeable needle set manufacturers usually offer additional needle tips and cables for separate purchase. However, design limitations prevent interchangeable sets from including needles smaller than a US 4; below that size, the needles are too fine to be connected with an interlocking mechanism.

Other details vary between sets. Some allow the knitter to join multiple cables together to increase the length of the needles (great for knitting very large circumferences or for trying on a sweater knit in the round). Most come in a case that's useful for transporting your tools. All sets have caps that you can place on the ends of a cable to create a long stitch holder or use to convert the circular needles to very long "straight" needles (a cable with a needle tip on one end and an end cap on the other).

Interchangeable needle sets are available at a range of price points from the very affordable Denise plastic set to the luxurious Lantern Moon Ebony set. My favorites are WEBS Interchangeable Bamboo Needles and Addi Turbo Clicks. An interchangeable needle set can be a great value. For an initial investment of about $50 to $200, you are buying the equivalent of about 27 circular needles. Also, buying one of these sets means that you always have the right needle on hand for the job.

With so many yarns to choose from, it's easy to be overwhelmed. Here is some basic information about yarn to get you started.

BALL BAND INFORMATION

The ball band is the label that comes on a ball or skein of yarn. This label gives information such as the manufacturer, name of the yarn, fiber content, yardage, weight, washing instructions, and suggested gauge and needle size. It may also include the color and dye lot. When buying more than one ball of the same color, be sure to purchase yarn from the same dye lot.

YARN WEIGHT

Yarn is available in a variety of weights. Knitters interchangeably express yarn weight in terms of stitches per inch and its weight name. Some common yarns for knitting are:

1. lace (8.25–10 stitches/inch)

2. fingering (6.75–8 stitches/inch)

3. sport (5.75–6.5 stitches/inch)

4. DK (5.25–6 stitches/inch)

5. worsted (4–5 stitches/inch)

6. chunky (3–3.75 stitches/inch)

7. bulky (1.5–2.75 stitches/inch)

Shawls and other lacy items are often worked in lace- or fingering-weight yarn. Socks and baby garments are best knit in fingering-weight yarn. Fingering-weight yarn is also an excellent choice for detailed colorwork items. Sweaters are most often knit out of DK, worsted-weight, or chunky yarn. Bulky yarns are best for very warm outerwear. You can knit accessories such as hats, mittens, scarves, and bags in any weight of yarn to good effect.

FIBER

Yarn is also available in a variety of fiber types:

Wool and **wool blends** are the most common and are a good all-around choice. They are elastic, durable, and warm.

Mohair and **alpaca** are other commonly available animal fibers. They lack the elasticity of wool but have excellent heat-retaining properties.

Cotton yarns are strong and durable but lack the elasticity of some other fibers. They are good for warm-weather garments.

Acrylic, sometimes manufactured to replicate the qualities of wool, is a good alternative if you are allergic to animal fibers. It is strong and somewhat elastic, but lacks the warmth of wool.

PLY

Yarns are made up of spun strands of fibers. Each strand of spun fiber is called a *ply*. Plied yarns are made up of multiple strands of these spun fibers, while single-ply yarns are made of only one strand. If you cannot find information about the number of plies on the yarn label, you can pull out an inch from one end of the ball, untwist the plies, and count them.

You can use any type of yarn for circular knitting, but some types are better than others for learning purposes. To learn circular (or any) knitting techniques, I recommend the following:

- **Work with a worsted-weight yarn.** Its size makes it perfect for learning new techniques. Thinner yarns can be fiddly and difficult to manipulate; thicker yarns can obscure stitches.

- **Work with a smooth yarn.** For learning, it's best to avoid textured, nubby, or furry yarns. It is very important when learning a new technique to be able to see your stitches clearly. Any yarn that obscures your stitches is not a good choice.

- **Work with a three- or four-ply yarn.** This type of yarn has the kind of stability you need when learning. Single-ply yarns tend to untwist as you knit with them. This can cause the yarn strand to separate and sometimes even break. Yarns with more than four plies usually have very fine strands that can separate and snag on your needles as you knit.

- **Work with wool yarn.** Wool is elastic, which makes it forgiving of a beginner's uneven tension. Also, wool's durability allows you to rip it out and reknit it multiple times. Avoid cotton yarns when learning because they are inelastic and can be slippery. If you are allergic to wool, choose a good-quality acrylic.

- **Work with a light-colored yarn.**
Darker colors absorb the light around them and can make it difficult to see the details of your stitches. Lighter colors reflect light back to your eye. White can be too bright, but a light neutral color, such as natural or tan, is excellent, as are pastels.

Some yarns to consider include Cascade 220, Valley Yarns Northampton, Lion Wool, and Patons Classic Wool. If you have a wool allergy, then consider a good-quality acrylic or acrylic blend, such as Berroco Comfort, Lion Cotton-Ease, or Patons Canadiana.

Other Tools You Will Need

There are some basic knitting tools that every knitter should have on hand. Having the right tools helps you to be prepared for any knitting situation. Try to keep your tools separate from similar household items—you don't want your knitting scissors or tape measure disappearing into the family junk drawer. With all your tools assembled, you're ready to begin!

SCISSORS AND SEAMING NEEDLES

A sharp pair of small scissors, sometimes called *snips,* or some other form of yarn cutter is very important. Snips are my preferred cutting tool; however, Clover's round pendant yarn cutter is particularly handy for travel or for use around small children.

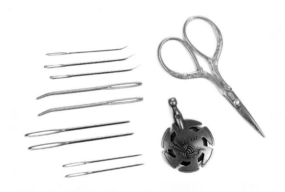

Seaming, or darning, needles are essential for both seaming and reserving stitches.

STITCH HOLDERS

Stitch holders are great for reserving stitches that are not currently being worked. For instance, when knitting a mitten, you might put the thumb stitches on a holder while you complete the hand portion of the mitten. Later, you would move the thumb stitches back to the needles to complete the thumb. I like to use scrap yarn instead of stitch holders; not only is the yarn more flexible, but I also usually have some lying around. A smooth yarn in a contrasting color works best.

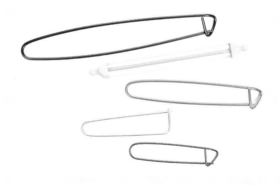

STITCH MARKERS

Stitch markers come in a variety of shapes, sizes, and materials. You can use them for marking off stitch repeats, for designating where increases or decreases occur, or even for reminding you when you have reached the end of a round (especially important in circular knitting). I prefer to use locking stitch markers, as you can also use them for holding pieces in place during seaming. Clover's are my favorite. There are also a number of cute novelty markers available, which do their job while making you smile, and are therefore worth a look.

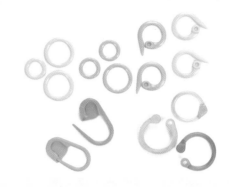

MEASURING TOOLS

A retractable tape measure is my favorite tool for measuring the length of knitted items. They are inexpensive, flexible, and readily available. They come in a variety of shapes from simple, round tape measures to novelty shapes.

A needle and stitch gauge is handy both as a measuring device for determining gauge and to ensure that you're using needles of the correct size. These range from the simple Susan Bates Knit Chek to Goose Pond's brass sheep-shaped gauge, among others. Choose a gauge that has at least a 2-inch measuring window.

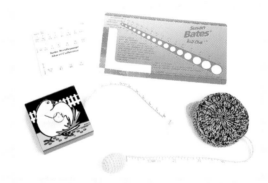

CROCHET HOOK

You should have at least one crochet hook, even if you can't crochet. A size E hook is a good all-purpose tool. You can use it for fixing mistakes, such as dropped stitches, or for picking up stitches along the edges of your work.

ROW COUNTERS

It's important to have on hand a pen and paper or a row counter to keep track of your work. Row counters are available in a variety of types. The simplest is a rotating counter that sits directly on your knitting needle. After each round, you turn a small dial to change the current round count in a small window. Clover makes a counter called a Kacha-Kacha that is quite a bit larger, and you click it each time you work a round. There are even a few row-counting applications available for smart phones!

CABLE NEEDLES

A cable needle is a short needle that you use to temporarily hold a small set of stitches out of the way while you work the next set of stitches. You work the stitches on the cable needle next, creating a twisted portion of knitting called a *cable*. Cable needles come in different sizes, shapes, and materials. The size of the cable needle should be the same as or smaller than your working needles. If you don't have a cable needle, a double-pointed needle of the same or smaller size can easily serve as a substitute.

KNITTING STORAGE

You can keep everything in one easily accessible location by using a knitting bag, bin, or toolbox. Storage for your tools and projects does not need to be expensive; simple, economical plastic bins make excellent storage. A tote bag for carrying your knitting with you is handy, but it does not need to cost a great deal. For example, you can reclaim a discarded purse or diaper bag and turn it into a knitting tote.

YARN CONTAINERS

It is important to manage your yarn while working on a project. Again, although there are containers created with the sole purpose of managing your yarn and keeping it clean and safe, you can recycle or repurpose many household items to hold yarn. The container should allow the yarn to move freely off of the ball while protecting it from dirt and dust and curious hands or paws.

MATERIALS FOR TAKING NOTES

A few basic office supplies are handy for taking notes, planning projects, and tracking changes that you have made to an existing pattern. Self-stick note pads make referencing different pages of books or magazines much simpler. Colored pencils and graph paper help with planning stripes or colorwork projects. It is important to take notes as you work so that you can re-create any changes you've made as well as make note of any tricky areas you come across when working with a pattern.

TIP

There are so many options available for knitting bags and containers that it is easy to feel overwhelmed. Take your time, talk to other knitters, and make a good investment. I have had my favorite bag, a Lexie Barnes Lady B, for five years and I still love it.

CHAPTER 2

Circular Knitting Methods

Now that you understand how circular knitting differs from flat knitting and you know a little about the tools required, it's time to learn how to knit in the round. There are four main methods of circular knitting: one uses double-pointed needles, while the other three make use of one or more circular needles but in different ways. After reading through these techniques, you can try them out with the starter projects in Chapter 4.

Cast On for Circular Knitting

Casting on for circular knitting is really the same as casting on for flat knitting—in both cases you make a series of loops on one of your needles. These loops serve as the foundation for your later rounds of knitting. The steps below demonstrate the long-tail cast-on, which is a flexible and attractive cast on that works well for most projects. For information about other types of cast-ons, see the Appendix.

Long-Tail Cast-On

To estimate how much yarn you need for your cast-on, follow steps 1 and 2 below.

① Hold one needle (double-pointed or circular) in your right hand with the tip pointing to the left. Leaving a tail about 6 inches long, wrap the yarn once around the needle for each stitch that you want to cast on.

② Make a slipknot in the working yarn beyond the point where you created the last wrap. Remove the wraps from the needle and place this slipknot on the needle.

NOTE: This slipknot counts as your first cast-on stitch.

③ Hold the needle with the slipknot in your right hand. Place your right index finger on top of the loop on this needle to hold the yarn in place. There are now two strands of yarn hanging down from the needle: one is the working yarn attached to the ball, and the other is the long tail. Arrange these strands so that the tail is toward you and the working yarn is to the back.

④ Grasp both strands in your left hand, holding them with your last three fingers. Then use your thumb and index finger to separate the strands into a diamond shape.

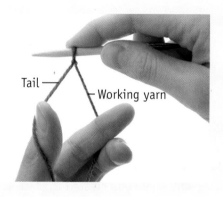

Tail

Working yarn

⑤ Still holding the yarns as above, turn your left hand so that your palm is facing you.

6 Move the tip of the needle below the loop of yarn on your thumb. Slide the needle under and up into this loop.

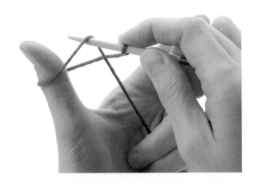

7 Continue to move the needle up and bring it over the strand of yarn on your left index finger.

8 Catch this strand of yarn on your needle tip and bring it back down through the loop on your thumb.

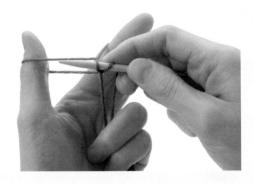

9 Let the loop fall off your thumb. Then gently pull both yarn strands down to tighten the stitch into place.

NOTE: As with any cast on, do not tighten this stitch too much. It should slide comfortably on your needle but should not appear sloppy.

10 Repeat steps 4–9 until you have cast on the correct number of stitches for your project.

TIP

For an attractive and flexible cast-on edge, it is important to space the cast-on stitches evenly as you tighten them on the needle. Leave a small gap between the stitches—they should be a little more than a stitch-width apart. Doing so will prevent your cast-on edge from being too tight.

Incorrect

Work with Double-Pointed Needles

The oldest method of knitting in the round involves using double-pointed needles (dpns)—straight needles that are tapered at both ends. They are available in all standard sizes and a range of lengths, which allows you to knit a variety of smaller-circumference items.

Overview

Double-pointed needles come in sets of four or five. To work with them, you set aside one of the needles and divide your stitches among the remaining three or four. You use the free needle to knit the set of stitches on the first needle. After you have worked that set of stitches, the first needle becomes the free needle, and you use it in turn to work the next set of stitches. That may sound complicated, but it is really quite simple, as you will see below.

Double-pointed needles are most often used to knit small circumferences, such as socks, mittens, gloves, the tops of hats, and the cuffs of sleeves. You can use this method to knit larger circumferences if you use longer needles or work with more than the four or five dpns that come in a set. You can use as many needles as you need to work comfortably around the circumference of your project. However, most knitters prefer to use no more than five needles at a time, since it can become unwieldy.

See the "Needles for Circular Knitting" section of Chapter 1 for more information and recommendations about double-pointed needles.

Pros and Cons of Working with Double-Pointed Needles

- Double-pointed needles are good for knitting small circumferences. They are particularly good for working on very narrow tubes, such as the fingers of gloves and the thumbs of mittens (a), which are not as well suited to the other methods.

- Projects that you work on with double-pointed needles are not as portable as those that you work on with the other circular methods. The stitches can easily slip off the ends of the needles, and the multiple needle points tend to poke holes through project bags. However, you can put end caps on the needles to keep the stitches in place, and special holders are made for traveling with dpns (b).

- Double-pointed needles seem to be more prone to laddering than the other methods of circular knitting (c). However, there are solutions for this (see the "Avoiding Ladders" section in Chapter 3).

- When working with double-pointed needles, it's very easy to accidentally pull on the wrong needle and unseat a whole needle's worth of stitches. This is a classic "oh no" moment, but you can quickly pick those stitches back up.

- Since there are so many needles to keep track of when working with double-pointed needles, it's easy to lose one of them. I have lost several between the seats of my car. Then you have to buy a new set (unless you are lucky, and it was a set of five). However, orphaned dpns can serve as impromptu cable needles or makeshift stitch holders.

- Accidentally dropping a metal double-pointed needle when knitting in public can attract a lot of attention with its loud noise. Depending on the situation, this could be a good thing or a bad thing.

a

b

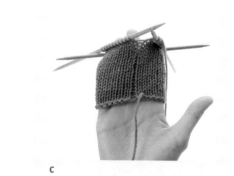

c

Working in the Round with Double-Pointed Needles

1 Following the instructions in the "Cast On for Circular Knitting" section on page 28, cast the desired number of stitches for your project onto one of your double-pointed needles.

2 Starting with the first cast-on stitch (the slipknot), move about one-third of the stitches onto an empty double-pointed needle. This is *needle 1*.

NOTE: When arranging stitches on the needles, be sure to slip the stitches as if to purl.

3 Slip the center one-third of the stitches onto another empty needle, now called *needle 2*. *Needle 3* retains the last one-third of the stitches. One empty needle *(needle 4)* remains.

NOTE: For a set of four double-pointed needles, you distribute the cast-on stitches among three of the needles (see photo). For a set of five double-pointed needles, you distribute the stitches among four of the needles. You use the remaining needle to work the first set of stitches.

④ Place the work on a table in front of you and take a look. The yarn tail and working yarn should be on your left. Needle 1 should be on your right.

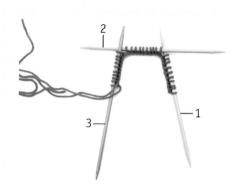

⑤ Adjust your cast-on edge so that it is not twisted around the needles. Make sure that the bottom edge of the cast on runs smoothly from needle to needle without looping over the needles.

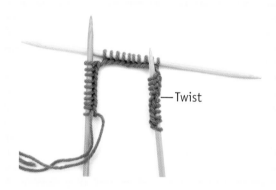

⑥ Flip the work over so that needle 3 (with the yarn tail and working yarn) is on the right, and needle 1 (with the first cast-on stitch) is on the left. Bring the free ends of needles 1 and 3 together to form a triangle. Lift the work in your left hand with needle 1 on top of needle 3. This may feel fiddly at first, but you will get used to it.

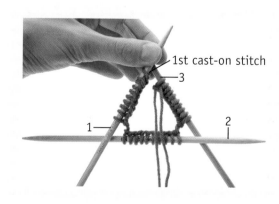

7 Position the working yarn so that it runs up from the last cast-on stitch to the outside of this triangle. The working yarn should not pass through the center of the triangle.

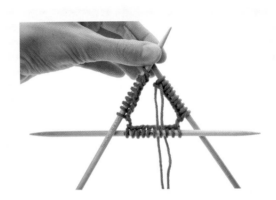

8 Begin to work in the round by inserting the tip of the empty needle (needle 4) into the first cast-on stitch on needle 1. Knit this stitch. Be sure to pull this first stitch tightly, as it will join your work.

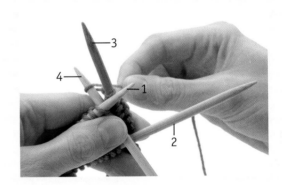

9 Continue knitting across needle 1. When you have knit all of the stitches on this needle, rotate your work and begin knitting the stitches of needle 2 using the newly emptied needle.

NOTE: Be sure to maintain a firm tension when knitting the first stitch on each needle. This helps to prevent laddering (see the "Avoiding Ladders" section in Chapter 3 for more details).

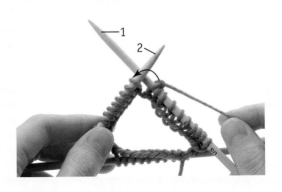

⑩ When you reach the end of needle 2, rotate your work again and use the empty needle to knit the stitches on needle 3.

⑪ When you reach the end of needle 3, you have knit one complete round. Note the presence of your yarn tail, which indicates where your new round begins. Because it gets harder to see the tail as you knit more rounds, you can use a stitch marker to indicate the end of your round (see Tip below).

⑫ Check that your work is not twisted—the cast-on runs smoothly along the bottom edge of your work and does not loop over the needles at any point. If you find a twist, see the "Correct a Twisted Cast-On" section in Chapter 3.

⑬ Repeat steps 8–11, continuing to knit in a spiraling path around your work.

11

TIP

Although your yarn tail will always help you identify the end of the round, it becomes harder to spot as you knit more rounds and the tail gets farther away from the needles. It is therefore a good idea to use a stitch marker to more clearly designate the end of the round. You can insert a locking or split-ring marker directly into the last stitch of the round and move it up every 20 rounds or so as needed. If you wish to use a solid-ring marker, place it before the last stitch of the round to keep it from falling off.

NOTE: Make certain that you are knitting around the *outside* of the tube you are creating. The right (knit) side should be to the outside and the wrong (purl) side to the inside. To correct this, just turn your work right-side out and begin working around the outside of the tube.

Correct

⑭ When your project has reached the desired length, bind off your work as shown in the "Bind Off in the Round" section later in this chapter.

TIP

Some knitters find working with double-pointed needles more difficult than other circular knitting techniques because of the number of needles involved. If you find starting with this method frustrating, try knitting back and forth on two needles for about 1 inch, and then divide the stitches onto multiple needles and join for working in the round. Continue working until you are comfortable, then rip the work out and begin again, this time joining the work immediately after the cast on.

A circular needle consists of two tapered needles (referred to here as **needle tips**) connected by a flexible cable. These needles were created to provide an alternative to double-pointed needles when knitting in the round.

Using the traditional method of knitting in the round with a circular needle, you cast the stitches on to one circular, distribute them evenly around the entire needle, and then slide them along the cable as you work in a continuous spiral around the outside of your project.

Overview

Chunky-weight project on one circular needle

Fingering-weight project on one circular needle

Circular needles come in many lengths to accommodate different-sized projects. When working with this technique, most knitters prefer to use a needle that is at least two inches shorter than the circumference of their project. However, if the needle is significantly shorter than the circumference of your project, your stitches will be crowded on the needle and difficult to work. This depends on the thickness of your yarn; the thinner your yarn, the more stitches you can fit around a circular of a given length. For example, you might be able to fit a shawl's worth of stitches in a lace-weight yarn onto a 16-inch circular, but that length needle would be difficult to use for an extra-large sweater that you worked in worsted-weight yarn.

As I mentioned in Chapter 1, circular needles come in lengths as short as 9 inches. These needles are designed to allow you to knit small-circumference items such as mittens or socks. However, I do not recommend the use of these tiny circulars, as they put a great deal of strain on the muscles of the hands and wrists. See the "Needles for Circular Knitting" section of Chapter 1 for more information as well as recommendations on circular needles.

For items that decrease to a central point (such as hats or bags), you can start on one circular needle and switch to double-pointed needles (or another method) when they get too small to fit comfortably around the circumference of the needle.

For items that you start from a small center and work outward (such as circular shawls or afghans), you can begin on double-pointed needles and move to a circular needle as soon as the stitches fit around the needle. Although it is possible to fit an item smaller than 16 inches on a 16-inch circular, I do not generally recommend it. Doing this stretches out the stitches along the cable and therefore can affect your gauge.

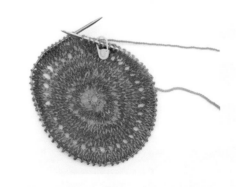

The Pros and Cons of Using One Circular: Traditional Method

- One circular works very well for medium- to large-circumference projects. It's ideal for skirts, pillow covers, ponchos, and the bodies of pullovers that you work in the round. It also works well for the main portion of hats, bags, and other items that decrease or increase from a central point.

- Working with one circular eliminates the need to rearrange your stitches or your needles at various points of the round, as occurs with all of the other three methods described here. Using one circular in the traditional method can be very fast since you never have to waste time changing needles. However, you do spend time sliding your stitches along the cable.

- Unlike the other methods of circular knitting, working in the traditional method on one circular needle virtually eliminates the possibility of laddering (see Chapter 3 for details about laddering). This is because there are no joins between the needles.

- Circular projects that you knit in this way are very portable; just slide the work completely onto the cables and away from the tips, tuck the work into a bag, and you are ready to go. The stitches are unlikely to slide off the ends of the needles unless they are very crowded on the circular, which probably indicates that you should be using a longer needle.

- When working in the round with one circular needle, it is easy to stop anywhere in the middle of a round. You can put down your work with a second's notice and not have to worry about leaving it in a precarious state. However, with the other methods, it is usually best to work to the end of a needle or side before stopping.

- When you are knitting a round in one continuous circuit, you can place stitch markers at any location in the round (anywhere along the way) and there is no risk of them falling off the ends of the needle.

- Because you are working with only one needle, there are no loose needles to lose or drop as with double-pointed needles.

- A drawback of the traditional circular method is that you may need many different lengths of needle in each size for various applications: shorter circulars for hats and baby sweaters, medium circulars for children's garments, and longer circulars for full-sized adult garments.

- One disadvantage of this method is that it is not suitable for use with small circumferences. Most knitters find very short circulars (9- and 12-inch) uncomfortable to work with and prefer to use another method of circular knitting for small items.

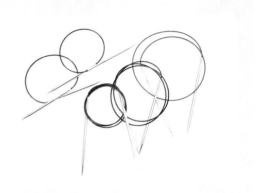

Working in the Round with One Circular: Traditional Method

1 Follow the instructions in the "Cast On for Circular Knitting" section earlier in this chapter to cast on the desired number of stitches for your project on the appropriate-length circular needle.

2 Slide the stitches along the cable so that they are evenly distributed along the entire length of the circular needle, being careful not to let them slip off either end of the needle.

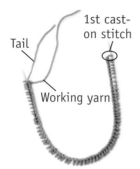

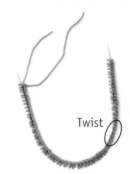

3 Lay the work down on a table in front of you and take a look. The yarn tail and working yarn should be on the left end of the circular needle, and the first cast-on stitch should be on the right end.

4 Adjust your cast-on edge so that it is not twisted around the needle. Make sure that the bottom edge of the cast-on runs smoothly from one end of the circular needle to the other without looping over the needles.

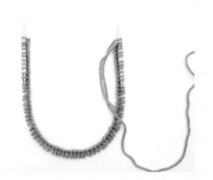

5 Flip the work over so that the needle tip with the yarn tail and working yarn is on the right and the needle tip with the first cast-on stitch is on the left. Bring the needle tips together to form a circle, being careful not to twist your cast-on edge.

6 Hold the work in your left hand, maintaining a grip on both needle tips. The left needle tip should be on top of the right needle tip.

7 Position the working yarn so that it runs up from the last cast-on stitch to the outside of the circle. The working yarn should not pass through the center of the circle.

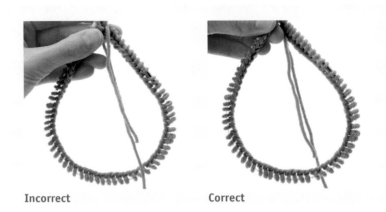

Incorrect   Correct

8 Begin to work in the round by inserting the tip of the right needle into the first cast-on stitch on the left needle and knitting it. Be sure to pull this first stitch tightly, as it will join your work.

9 Continue knitting the stitches on the left needle, sliding them along the cable as needed. Knit around on all stitches until you reach the end of the round, as indicated by the presence of the yarn tail. Place a stitch marker on your right-hand needle to clearly indicate the end of the round.

TIP

A stitch marker is especially useful with the traditional method of circular knitting, as there are no needle ends to remind you that you have reached the end of your round.

⑩ At this point, stop and check again that your work is not twisted. Verify that the cast on runs smoothly along the bottom edge of your work and does not loop over the needle at any point. If you find a twist, see the "Correct a Twisted Cast on" section in Chapter 3.

⑪ Continue to knit in a spiral path, moving the stitches along the cable as needed.

NOTE: Make certain that you are knitting around the *outside* of the tube you are creating. The right (knit) side should be to the outside and the wrong (purl) side to the inside. To correct this, just turn your work right-side out and begin working around the outside of the tube.

Correct

Incorrect

⑫ When your project has reached the desired length, bind off your work as shown in the "Bind Off in the Round" section later in this chapter.

Work with One Long Circular Needle: Magic Loop Method

Made popular in 2002 by Bev Galeskas and Sarah Hauschka in *The Magic Loop: Working Around on One Needle*, the magic loop method enables you to work projects of small circumference on one long circular. With this method, you pull out a loop of cable to divide your stitches, usually into two equal parts. Once you divide your stitches, you can use the free needle tip to knit across half of the stitches. You then rotate the project and work the remaining stitches.

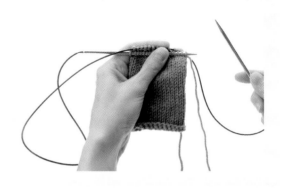

Overview

Most knitters find that a 32-inch circular is the shortest needle comfortable for the magic loop method. With this length circular, you can construct a sock, mitten, or other small-circumference item. However, I believe that a 40-inch circular is more useful, as you can use it for all of those items as well as for sleeves or the body of a child's sweater.

Circulars are available in lengths as long as 60 inches, but they can be difficult to find. You can use these longer needles with the magic loop method to knit larger items, such as the body of an adult sweater, but such a long cable may be awkward for smaller items. For more information and recommendations about circular needles, see the "Needles for Circular Knitting" section in Chapter 1.

46

You can even use the magic loop method to knit more than one item at once. In fact, I have written two books on this topic, *2-at-a-Time Socks* and *Toe-Up Two-at-a-Time Socks*, both of which explain how to knit two socks at once on a 40-inch circular.

The Pros and Cons of the Magic Loop Method

- The greatest benefit to the magic loop method is that you can knit many different circumferences with one long needle. This eliminates the need to buy needles in different lengths; one 40-inch circular needle can replace a 16-, 24-, and sometimes even a 32-inch needle for many knitting projects.

- Projects knit using this method are extremely portable. When you need to move or store your work, simply slide the entire project onto the cable. The work is then safely held on the cable, and there is no chance of dropped or lost stitches when you fold the project into your knitting bag. When you want to knit again, just redivide the stitches by pulling out the cable loop.

- Another advantage to the magic loop method is that when you knit small-circumference items such as socks or mittens, it is very easy to try them on while they are in progress to check the fit. If you knit these items on double-pointed needles, you have to slide the stitches onto waste yarn in order to be able to try them on.

- Also, because you are working with only one needle, there are no loose needles to lose or drop as with double-pointed needles.

● This method works best with circular needles that have very flexible cables, such as any type of Addi circulars, Inox Express, or KA (see Chapter 1 for recommendations). However, more companies are improving the flexibility of their cables, so this is becoming less of an issue.

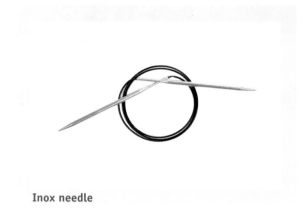

Inox needle

● When first learning this method, some knitters tend to lose the loop of cable that divides their stitches. If this happens to you, be sure that you always slide the front set of stitches onto the front needle before pulling the back needle. If the problem persists, try using a longer circular or pull more gently when sliding your stitches on the needles.

● If you pinch a cable too firmly when dividing your stitches, you can leave a permanent kink in your cable. However, as you become more accustomed to using this method, you will learn how to gently tease the cable out rather than pinching it.

Working in the Round with the Magic Loop Method

① Follow the instructions in the "Cast On for Circular Knitting" section earlier in this chapter to cast on the desired number of stitches for your project on one 40-inch circular needle.

② Slide the stitches to the right so that they are all positioned on the cable portion of the circular needle.

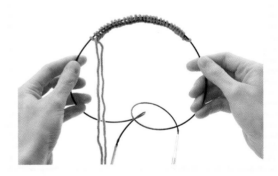

③ Lay the work down on a table in front of you and take a look. The yarn tail and working yarn should be on the left, and the first cast-on stitch should be on the right.

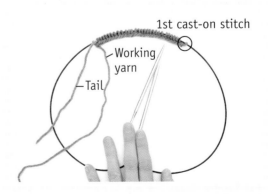

1st cast-on stitch

Working yarn

Tail

④ Adjust your cast-on edge so that it is not twisted around the needle. Make sure that the bottom edge of the cast on runs smoothly along the cable without looping over the needle.

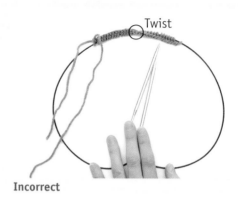

Twist

Incorrect

⑤ Flip the work over so that the end of the needle with the yarn tail and working yarn is on the right and the end with the first cast-on stitch is on the left.

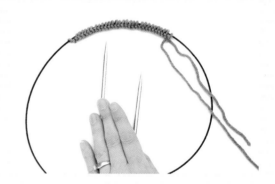

⑥ Count across half of the stitches. Carefully separate the stitches at this spot and pull about 6 to 8 inches of the cable through the opening, dividing the stitches in half.

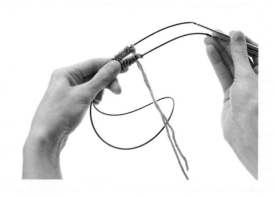

7 Fold your work in half so that both needle tips are pointing to the right and the section containing the first cast-on stitch is in front (facing you). Again check that your cast-on edge is not twisted around the needles.

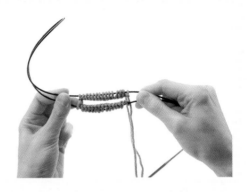

8 Position the working yarn so that it runs up from the last cast-on stitch to the outside of the project. The working yarn should not pass through the center of the project.

9 Hold your work in your left hand and slide the front set of stitches (the set containing the first cast-on stitch) to the right until they are resting on the needle. Then take the empty back needle in your right hand and bring it into position to knit.

⑩ Knit into the first stitch on the left-hand needle; this will join your work. Then knit across the remaining stitches on the left-hand needle.

NOTE: Keep your first stitch or two tight to prevent a gap from forming between your needles.

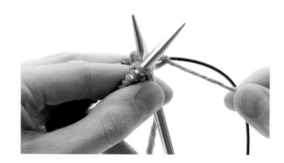

⑪ Rotate your work so that the set of unworked stitches is now facing you.

⑫ Again, slide the front set of stitches to the right until they are resting on the needle. Then slide the back set of stitches to the left so they are resting on the back portion of the cable.

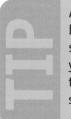

TIP

Always be sure to keep a loop of cable between your two sets of stitches. If you should lose this loop of cable, simply divide your work in half again by pulling the cable through the stitches at the appropriate spot.

⓭ Using the now-empty back needle, knit across the front set of stitches. Remember to keep the first stitch tight.

⓮ When you reach the end of these stitches, you will have worked one complete round. Note the presence of your yarn tail, which indicates where your new round begins. Use a stitch marker to indicate the beginning of your round if desired (see Tip below).

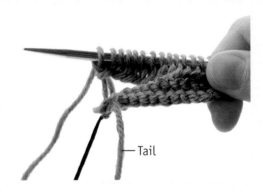

— Tail

TIP

Although your yarn tail will always help you identify the end of the round, it becomes harder to spot as you knit more rounds and the tail gets farther away from the needles. It is therefore a good idea to use a stitch marker to more clearly designate the end of the round. You can insert a locking or split-ring marker directly into the last stitch of the round and move it up every 20 rounds or so as needed. If you wish to use a solid-ring marker, place it before the last stitch of the round to keep it from falling off.

⑮ At this point, stop and check again that your work is not twisted. Verify that the cast on runs smoothly along the bottom edge of your work and does not loop over the needles at any point. If you find a twist, see the "Correct a Twisted Cast On" section in Chapter 3.

⑯ Rotate your work again so that the stitches you are going to work next are facing you, slide the front stitches onto the needle tip and the back stitches onto the cable, and work across the front set of stitches. Continue on in this manner, rotating your work and arranging your stitches, after you have worked each side.

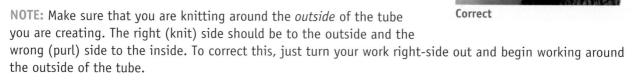

Correct

NOTE: Make sure that you are knitting around the *outside* of the tube you are creating. The right (knit) side should be to the outside and the wrong (purl) side to the inside. To correct this, just turn your work right-side out and begin working around the outside of the tube.

⑰ When your project has reached the desired length, bind off as shown in the "Bind Off in the Round" section later in this chapter.

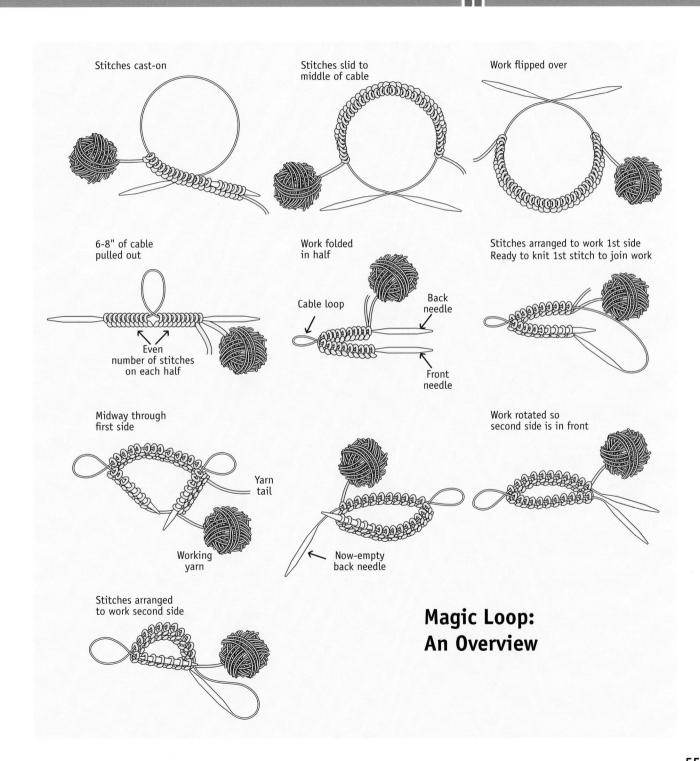

Stitches cast-on

Stitches slid to
middle of cable

Work flipped over

6-8" of cable
pulled out

Even
number of stitches
on each half

Work folded
in half

Cable loop

Back
needle

Front
needle

Stitches arranged to work 1st side
Ready to knit 1st stitch to join work

Midway through
first side

Yarn
tail

Working
yarn

Now-empty
back needle

Work rotated so
second side is in front

Stitches arranged
to work second side

Magic Loop:
An Overview

Work with Two Circular Needles

The final method of knitting in the round divides the project onto two circular needles, thus allowing you to knit a wide range of circumferences. Cat Bordhi first published a description of this technique in 2001 in her book *Socks Soar on Two Circular Needles*. This method is popular with some sock knitters.

Overview

With this method, you divide your stitches evenly between two circular needles and arrange them to form a circle. You knit the first half of the stitches using both needle tips of the front circular, and then knit the second half of the stitches using both needle tips of the back circular. In this way, you knit in a spiral around the outside of your work, while each set of stitches remains on the same circular needle.

When working with this method, most knitters use two circulars of the same length. However, the needles don't have to be the same length (see photo), just the same size. You can use whatever circulars you have on hand, as long as their combined length will comfortably accommodate the number of stitches in your project. To make your project as manageable as possible, it is best to use needles with shorter cables. For example, you can use two 16-inch circulars for a wide range of projects, from mitten thumbs to children's sweaters. For more information on circular needles, see the "Needles for Circular Knitting" section in Chapter 1.

The Pros and Cons of Working with Two Circulars

- One great thing about the two-circular method is that you can use it for any circumference, small or large. You can knit the finger of a glove with two 16-inch circulars, or you can knit a large circular shawl with two 40-inch circulars. If you divide your work among additional circular needles, you can work even larger circumferences.

- Projects knit using this method are extremely portable. When you need to move or store your work, simply slide the entire project onto the cable of the front and back needles. The work is then safely held on the cable, and there is no chance of dropped stitches when you fold the project into your knitting bag.

- Another advantage to the two-circular method is that when you knit small-circumference items such as socks or mittens, it is very easy to try them on while they are in progress to check the fit. If you knit these items on double-pointed needles, you would have to slide the stitches onto waste yarn in order to be able to try them on.

- One drawback of this method is that multiple needle tips dangling from your work can cause confusion. When starting to work a side, it can take a moment to distinguish which needle tip is which. This becomes easier as you become more familiar with this method. In the meantime, one solution is to put a dab of colored nail polish on both ends of one of the needles. This will help you distinguish between the front and back needles more easily.

- Another disadvantage is the need to have two circulars of the same size but not necessarily the same length. If you already own a lot of circulars, this won't be much of a drawback for you, but if you are just building your collection of needles, this can be a consideration. There is definitely a cost saving in using the other methods, which require only one circular needle or set of double-pointed needles. However, some knitters feel that no other method is quite as flexible.

Working in the Round with Two Circulars

① Follow the instructions in the "Cast On for Circular Knitting" section earlier in this chapter to cast the desired number of stitches for your project onto one of your circular needles.

2 Lay the work down on a table in front of you and take a look. The yarn tail and working yarn should be on the left, and the first cast-on stitch should be on the right.

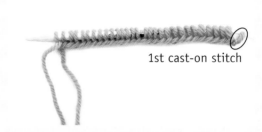

1st cast-on stitch

3 Adjust your cast-on edge so that it is not twisted around the needle. Make sure that the bottom edge of the cast on runs smoothly along the cable without looping over the needle.

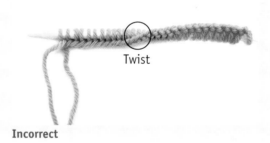

Twist

Incorrect

4 Flip the work over so that the end of the needle with the yarn tail and working yarn is on the right and the needle with the first cast-on stitch is on the left.

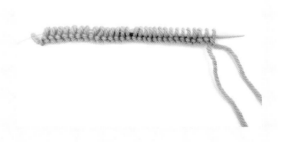

⑤ Starting with the last cast-on stitch, slip half of the stitches to the second circular needle.

NOTE: When moving the stitches between the needles, be sure to slip the stitches as if to purl.

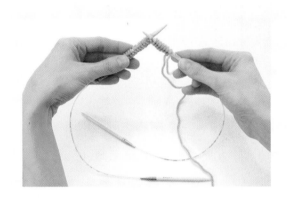

⑥ Fold your work in half so that the two circular needles are parallel to each other and the wrong sides of the cast-on edge are together. The needle containing the first cast-on stitch should be in front (facing you), and both sets of stitches should be at the left end of the circular needles. Again, check your work to ensure that your cast-on edge is not twisted around the needles.

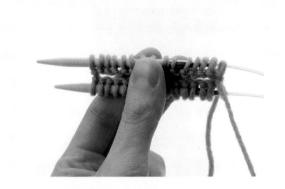

⑦ Slide both sets of stitches to the right onto the cable portion of their respective circular needles. Then, holding your work in your left hand, slide just the front set of stitches (the set containing the first cast-on stitch) further to the right until the front stitches are resting on the needle tip.

8 Position the working yarn so that it runs up from the last cast-on stitch to the outside of the project. The working yarn should not pass through the center of the project.

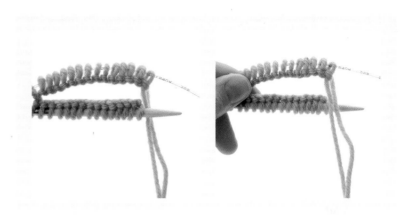

Incorrect placement of working yarn   *Correct placement of working yarn*

9 With your right hand, take the empty needle tip at the far end of the front circular needle and bring it into position to knit.

10 Knit into the first stitch on the front needle; this will join your work. Then knit across the remaining stitches on the front needle.

NOTE: Keep your first stitch or two tight to prevent a gap from forming between your needles.

11 Rotate your work so that the set of unworked stitches on the back circular is now facing you.

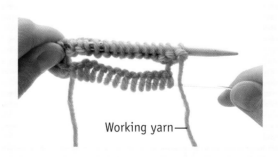

Working yarn—

⑫ Again, slide the front set of stitches to the right until they are resting on the needle. Then slide the back set of stitches to the left so they are resting on the cable of the back circular needle.

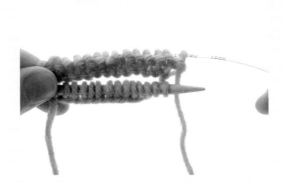

⑬ With your right hand, take the empty needle tip at the far end of the front circular needle and use it to knit the stitches on the front needle. Remember to keep the first stitch tight.

⑭ When you reach the end of these stitches, you will have worked one complete round. Note the presence of your yarn tail, which indicates where your new round begins. Use a stitch marker to indicate the beginning of your round if desired (see Tip below).

⑮ At this point, stop and check again that your work is not twisted. Verify that the cast on runs smoothly along the bottom edge of your work and does not loop over the needles at any point. If you find a twist, see the "Correct a Twisted Cast on" section in Chapter 3.

16 Rotate your work again so that the stitches you are going to work next are facing you, slide the front stitches onto the needle tip and the back stitches onto the cable, and work across the front set of stitches. Continue on in this manner, rotating your work and arranging your stitches after you have worked each side.

Make sure that you are knitting around the *outside* of the tube you are creating. The right (knit) side should be to the outside and the wrong (purl) side to the inside. To correct this, just turn your work right-side out and begin working around the outside of the tube.

Correct

TIP

Although your yarn tail will always help you identify the end of the round, it becomes harder to spot as you knit more rounds and the tail gets farther away from the needles. It is therefore a good idea to use a stitch marker to more clearly designate the end of the round. You can insert a locking or split-ring marker directly into the last stitch of the round and move it up every 20 rounds or so as needed. If you wish to use a solid-ring marker, place it before the last stitch of the round to keep it from falling off.

17 When your project has reached the desired length, bind off your work as shown in the "Bind Off in the Round" section later in this chapter.

Sometimes when using this method, you will accidentally knit the front set of stitches using the back needle instead of the front needle. You will know this has happened when you knit to the end of the front set of stitches and an empty needle suddenly falls in your lap. Your work may appear to be a twisted mess, but it is easily remedied. Just slip half of the stitches back onto the empty circular and you are ready to go.

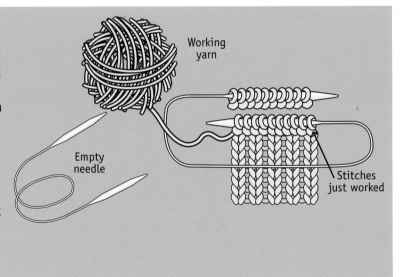

Working yarn

Empty needle

Stitches just worked

When you are done knitting in the round, you must bind off your project (also called *casting off*). One of the easiest and most versatile bind offs is the basic bind off. For information about other types of bind offs, see the Appendix. The steps below demonstrate this technique with one circular needle used in the traditional method. The procedure is the same for the other circular knitting methods.

Basic Bind Off

① Place a stitch marker on your right-hand needle to indicate the end of the round. Then knit the first two stitches of the round as usual. There are now two stitches on your right-hand needle to the left of the end-of-round marker.

NOTE: I used a contrasting color of yarn here to more clearly show the stitches being worked. When binding off your knitting, work the bind off with your project yarn.

TIP

Markers: To Use or Not to Use

Although a marker is helpful if you are using one circular in the traditional method, you may not need a marker with the other methods, as the end of the round usually occurs at the end of a needle.

② Using the tip of your left-hand needle, lift the first stitch of the round on the right-hand needle up and over the second stitch and off the right-hand needle. You have bound off one stitch, and one stitch remains on the right-hand needle to the left of the end-of-round marker.

③ Knit one more stitch, so that there are again two stitches on the right-hand needle to the left of the end-of-round marker. Then again lift the first stitch over the second and off the right-hand needle.

④ Repeat Step 3 until you reach the end of the round and one stitch remains on your right-hand needle (see photo).

TIP

Binding Off in Pattern

If your pattern instructs you to "bind off in pattern," instead of knitting each stitch before binding it off, just knit or purl it as necessary to continue the established stitch pattern.

⑤ Cut the yarn, leaving an eight-inch tail. Slip the
final loop off the needle and pull this loop up until
the yarn tail comes free and the loop no longer
remains.

⑥ Take a look at your bound-off edge and notice that
the bound-off stitches appear to be a series of over-
lapping *V*s that run horizontally along the edge of
your work.

⑦ Thread the yarn tail onto a seaming needle. Insert
the seaming needle from front to back under both
legs of the *V* that constitutes the first bound-off
stitch of the round. Pull the needle through and
snug up this stitch, but don't pull it so tight that
you distort the fabric.

⑧ Insert the seaming needle down into the middle of the last bound-off stitch (into the center of the *V*) and then back toward the center of the project. Pull the needle through and snug up the yarn so that this connector stitch is the same size as the surrounding bound-off stitches.

⑨ Weave in the yarn tail on the wrong side of the fabric as usual.

TIP

How to Bind Off More Loosely

For a looser bound-off edge, work the bind off using a needle that is one or two sizes larger than the needle you used for your project.

Now that you've been introduced to all four methods of knitting in the round, you may feel overwhelmed by your options. The table below should help clear up the differences between the techniques presented in this chapter.

Method	Needles	When to Use	Best for Items Such As
Double-pointed needles method	1 set of 4 or 5 dpns: short length for small-circumference projects, longer length for larger projects	Small circumferences	Socks, mittens, gloves (especially the fingers), cuffs of sleeves, crowns of hats, the bottoms of bags, the centers of circular shawls or afghans
One circular: traditional method	1 circular, slightly smaller in length than the circumference of the project	Medium to large circumferences (greater than 16 inches)	Skirts, ponchos, bodies of sweaters, hats (up to the crown), tote bags (usually excluding the bottom construction), pillow covers, the outer portion of circular shawls or afghans that are worked from the center outward
One long circular: magic loop method	1 long circular, 32 to 40 inches long	Small to medium circumferences	Socks, mittens, gloves, sleeves (including cuffs), bodies of children's sweaters
Two circular needles method	2 circulars of any length (they don't need to be the same length)	Small to large circumferences	Socks, mittens, gloves, sleeves (including cuffs), bodies of sweaters (especially when you want to try them on in progress)

CHAPTER 3

Special Techniques for Circular Knitting

There are some special techniques that can help make your circular knitting a breeze by offering solutions to sticky spots. This is by no means a complete offering of knitting tips and tricks, but it is an excellent starting point for knitters new to circular methods.

Knowing how to fix your knitting when problems arise really is necessary to a positive experience. There's nothing more frustrating than a problem you can't fix by yourself that requires you to rip out and restart your work. You can rely on these solutions when mistakes occur.

Knit on the Inside of the Tube

One mistake that first-time circular knitters make is knitting into the inside of the tube they are creating, rather than into the outside. The result is that their work is wrong-side out, with the wrong side of the project visible and the right side hidden inside the tube. In my teaching experience, about 10 percent of new circular knitters do this. It's not difficult to fix, but you do need to address it.

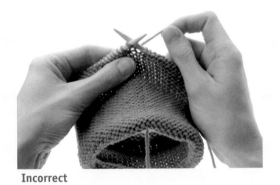

Incorrect

Correct

When working in stockinette, the knit (or right) side should be to the outside and the purl (or wrong) side should be to the inside. When working in the round correctly, you will always be knitting into the right side of your work, and that right side will always be the outside of the tube you are creating. If you find that you are knitting around the inside of the tube, just turn your work right-side out and begin working into the outside of the tube.

Correct a Twisted Cast on

In patterns that are written for circular knitting, you often see a phrase like "Join, being careful not to twist your stitches." It's very easy to make this error in your work if you are not careful to avoid it. The good news is that you can fix it as long as you discover it in the first round of your knitting.

Twisted

Before knitting the first stitch of the round to join your work, check to make sure that the ridge at the bottom of your cast-on does not loop over and around the cable of your circular needle. If the stitches are twisted around the cable, you have two options: either cast on again more carefully, or attempt to correct the error. To fix the twist, work to the end of the first round and then bring the work between the needle tips to untwist it. Check before proceeding to be sure that you have untwisted the work and have not inadvertently inserted a new twist.

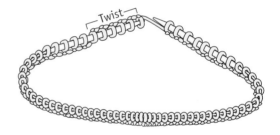

Then continue working in the round. Doing so will leave a small lump at the cast-on edge, but it's sometimes preferable to ripping out your work.

Avoid a Gap at the Join

You may have noticed that a small "notch" remains between your first and last cast-on stitches. You can tidy up this small gap when you weave in your yarn tail; however, there are ways to join your cast-on stitches that will prevent the gap from forming in the first place.

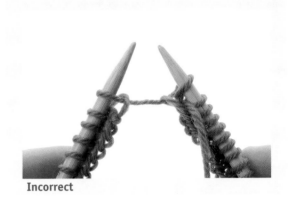

Incorrect

SWAP THE FIRST AND LAST CAST-ON STITCHES

① Cast on the desired number of stitches and arrange your needles for your chosen method of knitting in the round. Make sure that the working yarn is in the correct position to work the first stitch of the round: behind the needle tips if you will be working a knit stitch, or in front of the needles if you will be working a purl stitch.

1

② Move the first cast-on stitch (the slipknot) from the left-hand needle to the tip of the right-hand needle.

NOTE: When moving this stitch, slip it as if to purl so it does not twist.

2

③ Lift the second stitch (the last cast-on stitch) on the right needle over this slipped stitch (3a) and move it to the left-hand needle (3b). In this way, the first and last stitches of the round exchange places and close the gap that would otherwise form at the join.

④ Knit your first round as usual, starting with the first stitch on the left-hand needle.

3a

3b

CAST ON AN EXTRA STITCH AND DECREASE IT

① Cast on one stitch more than your desired number of stitches and arrange your needles in preparation to work in the round (see Chapter 2).

② Move the last cast-on stitch (the extra stitch) to the left-hand needle.

2

③ Knit together the first two stitches on the left-hand needle (the first cast-on stitch and the extra stitch). Doing so decreases away the extra stitch and tightly joins the work into a round.

3

WORK THE FIRST FEW STITCHES WITH BOTH STRANDS

① Cast on the desired number of stitches and arrange your needles in preparation to work in the round (see Chapter 2). Hold the working yarn and the yarn tail together to the inside of the work.

② With both strands held together, knit the first few stitches of the round. Then drop the yarn tail and finish working your project with just the working yarn.

FAQ

It is a good idea to practice all of the methods presented here for avoiding a gap at the join. You may find one method more comfortable than another, or you may decide to ignore all of my suggestions and tidy up this area with the yarn tail and a seaming needle when weaving in ends. Because there is no right or wrong way to perform this neatening of your work, whatever method feels most comfortable to you is the best.

PULL THE YARN TAIL THROUGH THE FIRST CAST-ON STITCH

1 Cast on the desired number of stitches and arrange your needles in preparation to work in the round (see Chapter 2). Using the yarn tail, knit the first cast-on stitch on the left-hand needle, but do not remove that stitch from the left-hand needle.

2 Pull up on the loop you created on the left-hand needle until the yarn tail comes through the stitch. Doing so "undoes" the stitch you just knit, but leaves the tail pulled through the first stitch. Gently tug on the yarn tail to tighten it.

3 Drop the yarn tail and use the working yarn to reknit the first cast-on stitch. Then knit to the end of the round as usual. Tighten up the join by tugging gently on the yarn tail.

Avoid Ladders

A *ladder* is a column of extended running threads that are surrounded on either side by normal stitches. They resemble the rungs of a ladder, hence the name. Laddering can happen in circular knitting in the area between the last stitch of one needle and the first stitch of the next. A ladder may be barely noticeable, or it may be so wide that it looks like a column of dropped stitches. In either case, it is neither attractive nor desirable.

Laddering is a particular problem when using double-pointed needles, but it can also happen with the magic-loop and two-circular-needle methods. Since laddering occurs only at the joins between needles, it does not happen when using one circular needle in the traditional method. If you are having a problem with laddering and can't use that method, try one of the solutions presented on the following pages.

Laddering

USE A SET OF 5 DPNS INSTEAD OF 4

Some knitters find that working with a set of five double-pointed needles instead of four helps to reduce laddering. It increases the angle at which the needles meet and thereby eases the tension on the stitches in these locations ensuring that less laddering will occur.

MAINTAIN TENSION WHEN SWITCHING NEEDLES

An easy way to reduce laddering is to pull the working yarn extra tight when working the first two stitches on *every* needle, as shown in the photo below. If you find that ladders are still present, you can also work the last two stitches on each needle tightly.

TWO CIRCULARS: KEEP THE BACK STITCHES ON THE CABLE

If you are experiencing laddering when working in the round with two circulars, make sure that the stitches on the back circular needle are on the cable (not the needle tip) before you work the stitches on the front needle. Doing so will allow you to pull the first stitch on the front needle tighter, which will help balance the tension between the two cables.

Incorrect

Correct

MOVE THE STITCHES BETWEEN THE NEEDLES

A popular remedy for laddering is to move the first few stitches on each needle to the previous needle after working every few rounds. This moves the location where the needles meet, thus moving the location of the ladder. I don't recommend this method because it doesn't actually eliminate the ladder; it just staggers it so it is no longer vertical. However, it does make the laddering slightly less noticeable.

TIP

Magic Loop: Keep the Cable Crossed

If you are working in the magic loop method and are having trouble with ladders, make sure that the cable crosses over itself at the base of each loop. The cross in the cable helps the stitches on either side of the loop stay closer together.

When working flat, you can join new yarn at the sides of a piece and weave the ends into the seam. In fact, most knitting books specify that you should try to join new yarn at the end of a row. You can waste a lot of yarn this way. There is nothing more frustrating than knitting to within an inch or two of the end of a row only to discover that you don't have enough yarn to finish. When working in the round, you can join yarn at any point. The benefit is that there is very little yarn waste, but you will need to find a way to hide the joining of new yarn invisibly that does not involve running it into a seam. Below are three options for hiding your yarn tails or joining new yarn in a way that results in no tail at all.

BASIC METHOD OF JOINING YARN

This simple method works with any yarn, but it may not be the best alternative. It leaves ends that must be woven in later, which can create additional bulk. Some knitters choose to change yarns at the sides of their work, but I feel that if you do it correctly, you can change yarns at any point and it will not be visible on the right side when you complete the work.

Work until you have 6 inches of yarn remaining. Simply begin knitting with your new ball of yarn (a contrasting color is shown here), leaving a 6-inch tail on it as well. The first few stitches may feel loose, so you may want to make a simple overhand knot to help hold the new yarn in place. Remove this overhand knot before you weave in your ends.

WEAVING IN ENDS

1. To weave in ends, make sure that the yarn is on the wrong side of the fabric. Thread the yarn tail onto a seaming needle.

2. On the wrong side, weave the needle and tail yarn across a row, under the purl bumps (sometimes called back loops) of the stitches. Do this for at least 4 stitches.

3. Move to the round below and weave back in the opposite direction. As a rule, I like to reverse directions at least twice, passing through at least 4 stitches per round.

Once you weave the yarn in, gently smooth the fabric into shape and then clip the yarn tail close to the fabric.

SPLICING YARNS (SPIT SPLICE)

This method is most appropriate for plied yarns. Although most sources recommend that you use it only for wool yarns, I have used it on a variety of nonsuperwash animal fibers without problems. As long as the yarn has a little "toothiness" to it, this method is effective. I do not recommend it for cotton, rayon, silk, or other slippery fibers.

1

❶ Work with your old yarn until a 6-inch tail remains. Untwist about 4 inches of both the old and the new yarn. Cut away 3 to 4 inches from half of the plies of each yarn.

❷ Overlap the uncut strands in your dominant hand and apply a little saliva to them. You can use water if the thought of spitting on your yarn makes you uncomfortable, but saliva contains proteins that help bind the fibers together.

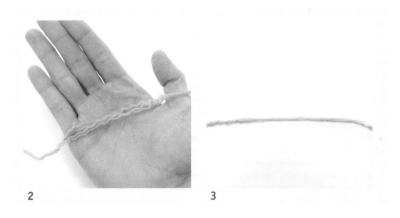

2   3

❸ Rub the overlapped strands between your palms to help bind and twist them together. You now have one continuous length of yarn with no added bulk and much less waste, and you can return to working in the round.

RUSSIAN JOIN

This method was only recently brought to my attention, and I have come to love it for any fiber that doesn't respond well to splicing (see above)—and even for some that do.

1 Work until you have about 6 inches of yarn remaining. Thread the old yarn onto a small seaming needle. Insert the needle back into the strand of yarn and weave it in and out of the plies for about 3 inches.

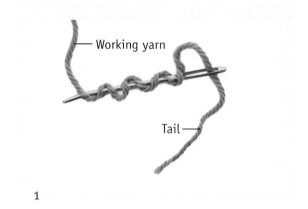

1

2 Pull the needle through, leaving a loop at the end of the old yarn. Remove the seaming needle for use on the next strand of yarn.

3 Now thread the needle with the new yarn and bring it through the loop you left in the old yarn, and then weave the needle in and out of the new yarn for 3 inches. Pull the needle through, creating a second loop that interlocks with the first.

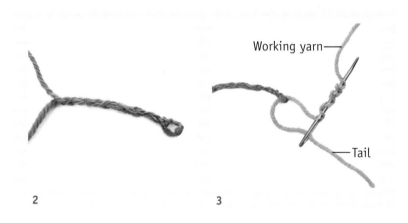

2   3

4 Pull gently on the tail ends of the old and the new yarn to tighten up the loops in both until you have what looks like a continuous strand of yarn.

5 Trim the old and new yarn tails close to the yarn strand. Return to working in the round, knitting right across the join you just created.

4

Knitting charts are often used for cables, colorwork, knit-and-purl combinations, and lace — combinations of stitches that add texture or color to a finished piece. Working charts in circular knitting is somewhat different than working charts in flat knitting. Knowing how to read charts will help enhance your knitting by giving you the flexibility to add drama to your work.

Most charts in stitch dictionaries are written for back-and-forth knitting. Each square of the chart represents one finished stitch. You begin in the lower right corner and work row 1 from right to left. Then you work row 2 from left to right, working each subsequent row in the opposite direction from the row before it. The arrows in the illustration at right show the direction in which you would work the first few rows. The row numbers are often shown alternately on both sides of the chart, indicating the beginning of each row. The key for this kind of chart often says something like "knit on the RS, purl on the WS." Directions written this way are a clear indicator for back-and-forth knitting.

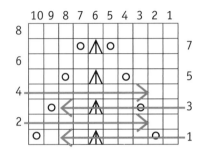

Flat knitting chart

When working a chart in the round, you are always working on the right side, so you work each row of the chart from right to left, and follow only the "RS" directions in the key. If a chart is intended to be worked in the round, it often shows row numbers only along the right side, and the key makes no reference to the "WS."

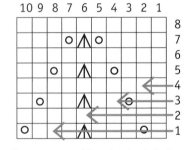

Chart converted for circular knitting

FYI

If a stitch pattern is written only in words, it is more difficult to work it in the round without charting it first. You need to work each wrong-side row backward while at the same time reversing each stitch (with a purl becoming a knit). Also, some techniques that you work on the wrong side are not easy to reverse, such as complex stitch manipulations in cables or lace patterns. I recommend that you first chart out any back-and-forth stitch pattern instructions and work in the round from that.

A *repeat* is a section of a chart that you work multiple times around or across your knitting. Some charts include partial repeats that you insert to center the pattern on a flat piece of knitting. You may want to remove these extra stitches when working in the round.

For example, the chart shown here has a six-stitch repeat (highlighted) with three stitches at the end to balance it. If you used this chart on a project worked flat, you would work the first six stitches repeatedly until you came to the last three stitches, where you would work the partial repeat at the end. However, when using this chart in the round, you would work only the high-lighted section around the circumference of the project.

You can keep track of where you are on a chart by placing a ruler beneath the line you are currently working. You can also use a highlighter or repositionable highlighter tape to divide the chart into ten-row segments for ease in finding your place, or simply cross out a row when you complete it. It is a good idea to photocopy your charts for marking on rather than marking directly in books. Photocopies also allow you to enlarge charts that are difficult to see.

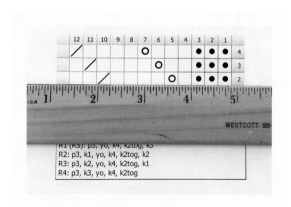

Tracking progress with a ruler

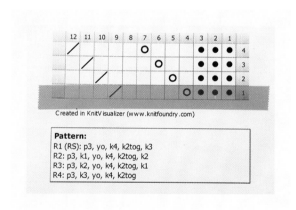

Tracking progress with repositionable tape

One of the most fun ways to spruce up a plain knitting project is to add color. However, working color in the round brings its own set of challenges. Here are some ideas for getting around them.

"JOGLESS" STRIPES

When working stripes in the round, a distinct offset of the pattern occurs at the beginning of a round, as shown at near right. This happens because you are creating a spiral that circles up to the top of the garment. Commonly called a "jog" in your work, it creates a bit of a jarring jump in the case of stripes. There are a few ways to eliminate this jog, as shown at far right. My personal favorite, the one I find the simplest to perform, is shown here, demonstrated on a simple striped swatch.

1 When you want to create a stripe, work to the end of the round with your current color of yarn (called color A here). Cut yarn A, leaving a 6-inch tail, and drop the tail to the inside of your work.

2 Pick up the yarn for your stripe (color B) and knit 1 stitch, leaving a 6-inch tail. Continue to knit with color B until you have worked 1 complete round.

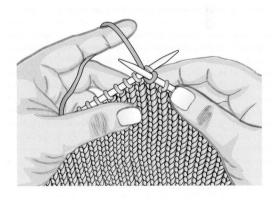

③ Insert the tip of the right-hand needle into the center of the stitch below the first stitch of color B (a). Lift this stitch onto the left-hand needle (b).

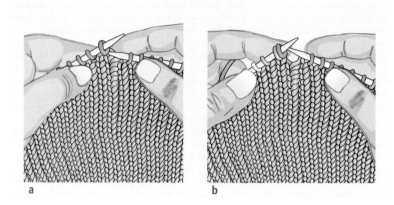

a

b

④ Knit the lifted stitch (in color A) and the next stitch (the first stitch of color B) together as shown in the photo. Then knit with color B normally to the end of the round. Continue working with color B for as many rounds as your pattern specifies.

⑤ Repeat steps 1–3 each time you want to work a round in a new color.

NOTE: This technique moves the end of the round one stitch to the left. This means that as you build a tube with many stripes, you will notice your beginning-of-round marker gradually drifting left away from your original cast-on tail.

TIP

When you are creating very thin stripes (only one or two rounds high and in only two colors), you can carry your yarn along the inside of your work instead of cutting it when changing colors. However, for thicker stripes, it is best to cut the old color before starting to work with the new color. Not cutting the yarn when carrying it up more than two rounds will create floats of yarn on the wrong side of your work that can catch on things and become loose and unattractive.

STRANDED KNITTING IN THE ROUND

Stranded colorwork involves knitting small patterns across the surface of your work, carrying colors as you go. It is actually much easier to work in the round than to work flat. In flat knitting, you have to work the pattern on both the right (knit) and wrong (purl) sides—and working colorwork on the wrong side is no picnic. You can't see the pattern clearly because the wrong side is facing you. Without the visual cue of the previous rows to guide you, it is easy to work a stitch in the wrong color.

One downside to working stranded colorwork in the round is that you will encounter jogs. You can use the method outlined in the previous pages for hiding the jog in stripes, but that can be difficult in a complicated pattern. If your colorwork chart includes a column of a single color, consider working the chart so that that column falls at the beginning or end of the round (a), which will make the jog less noticeable.

You can also modify your stitch pattern to add a narrow vertical stripe where the jog would be visible, such as at either side or the underarm of a sweater (b).

If none of those options appeals to you, then be sure to position the end of the round where the jog will be less visible. If you are knitting socks, let the end of the round fall at the back of the leg. If you are knitting mittens, put the end of the round on the side of the hand opposite the thumb.

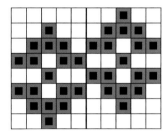

Simple stranded colorwork pattern showing jog at end of round
a

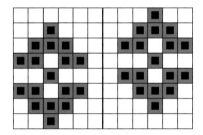

Color work chart with 2-stitch-wide vertical stripe separating color pattern on either side of end round
b

INTARSIA

Intarsia is a type of knitting that uses different colors to create a motif or pattern that involves large blocks of color. With very large blocks of color, it becomes impossible to strand the unused yarns along the back of the work, so instead, you introduce a new strand for each section of color. An example of intarsia is a sweater with a knitted-in picture of a ladybug in the center. You typically work this kind of knitting flat; it does not lend itself well to being worked in the round. If your heart is set on an intarsia pattern, I recommend that you work it flat rather than in the round.

Create False Seams

One of the benefits of working a sweater in the round is that there are no side seams to sew. However, some people feel that side seams improve the look and stability of a sweater. If you agree, it is possible to create the impression of a seam in a circular garment where a seam does not exist.

DROPPED-STITCH METHOD

One way to create a false seam is to drop a stitch and then work it back up the dropped-stitch column in an alternating pattern. This creates a column of elongated stitches that stands out subtly from the stitches around it. For this technique, you will need a crochet hook in the same size as your knitting needles.

① To create a false seam using this method, work to the last round of your garment, but do not bind off.

② Place a marker on the stitch at the top of the stitch column that you would like to become the "false seam."

③ Slip each stitch until you get to the marked stitch, and then drop the stitch all the way down to the round directly above the cast-on. There should be one stitch loop remaining at the bottom of the dropped column, with a ladder of running strands leading to the top of the work.

④ Insert the crochet hook into this loop, catch the first two running strands, and pull them through the stitch. Then catch the next single running thread and pull this through the loop on your hook. Alternate these two steps until you are back at the top of your work.

⑤ Place the "seam" stitch back onto the right-hand needle and continue to slip stitches until you get to the desired location of the next false seam or to the end of the round.

KNITTED-IN METHOD

Another way to create a false seam is to knit it into the garment as you go.

1 Before beginning your project, identify where you would like your false seams to occur. For example, on a pullover, you might want a stitch at the beginning of the round and a stitch on the opposite side of the garment.

2 After you cast on the stitches for your project, use markers to set those "seam stitches" off from the rest of the garment.

3 Then work these stitches in reverse stockinette or garter stitch while knitting the rest of the garment according to the pattern. Doing so will create the visual effect of a seam.

> **TIP**
>
> Before using one of these methods to create a false seam in a knitted garment, I recommend that you test each technique on a swatch made from your project yarn to ensure that you are satisfied with the finished appearance.

CHAPTER 4

Starter Projects

In order to increase your comfort level with the techniques presented in Chapter 2, it is a good idea to complete some simple projects before moving on to more complicated ones. This assemblage of three designs is just right for beginning circular knitters. Each is quick, easy, and useful, from a simple ear warmer and handy kitchen potholders to fingerless mitts.

ASSEMBLE YOUR MATERIALS

The projects in this chapter require only a few simple materials. First, you will need about 240 yards of worsted-weight yarn. You should also have on hand a variety of knitting needles so that you can practice each of the techniques in Chapter 2. Gather together the following needles, all in size US 8 (5mm):

- One set of 4 or 5 double-pointed needles

- Two 16-inch circular needles

- One 40-inch circular needle

You will also want to have a closed- or locking-ring stitch marker, a pair of scissors, and a seaming needle. Once you have your materials at hand, it's time to begin your starter projects!

DETERMINE YOUR GAUGE

Knit a swatch in stockinette using your chosen yarn and the recommended needle size (see the "Gauge and Swatching" section in Chapter 5). Next, measure your gauge in stitches per inch and compare this with the gauge specified for the project. The three projects featured in this chapter specify a gauge of 4 stitches per inch in stockinette. If you are getting more than 4 stitches per inch, make another swatch with a needle one size bigger. If you are getting fewer than 4 stitches per inch, make another swatch using a needle one size smaller. Once you achieve the specified gauge, proceed to the instructions for making your project.

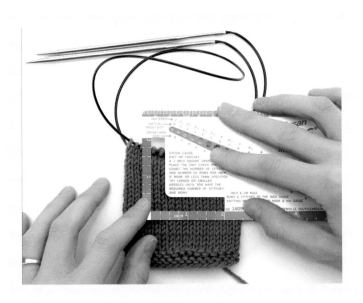

Simple Ear Warmer

Simple, useful, and attractive, this headband is a great accessory for cold or cool weather. This project knits up quickly and easily. Make one for yourself; make a few for gifts. Match them with the fingerless mitts later in this chapter and keep your head and hands toasty all season long. In order to complete both projects in the same yarn, you will need about 125 yards of worsted-weight yarn.

Specifications

SIZE
Finished dimensions: 15½ inches in circumference (unstretched) × 3 inches tall, to fit heads ranging from 20 to 23 inches around

MATERIALS
45 yards of worsted-weight yarn: Peace Fleece Worsted (70% wool/30% mohair, 200 yd./4 oz. skein), 1 skein in color Glasnost Gold, CYCA #4 (medium)

NEEDLES
You can use any of the following needles in size US 8 (5mm), or size to obtain gauge:

One 16-inch circular needle
One set of 4 or 5 double-pointed needles
One 32- to 40-inch circular needle
Two 16-inch circular needles

NOTIONS
Stitch markers
Seaming needle

GAUGE
4 stitches per inch in stockinette, worked in the round

Plan the Ear Warmer

CHOOSE A CIRCULAR KNITTING TECHNIQUE
You can work this project with any of the four circular knitting techniques covered in Chapter 2. It is so quick and easy that you may want to make four different ear warmers, each using a different technique.

CHOOSE YOUR YARN

Use any worsted-weight yarn that is soft and comfortable next to your skin. When selecting a yarn, you may find it useful to hold the skein against your cheek or neck and check for any irritation; these areas are more sensitive than your hands. If you want this ear warmer to be extra warm, be sure to select a yarn with a high percentage of wool or alpaca. Cotton yarns can be very soft, but they are not as warm.

Make the Ear Warmer

1. Cast on 72 stitches and arrange your work on the needles according to the directions for your chosen knitting method (see Chapter 2). Join your work to knit in the round, being careful not to twist your cast on around the needles. Place a stitch marker to indicate the end of the round.

2. *Knit 3, purl 1. Repeat from * to the end of the round.

3. Repeat Step 2 until your work measures about 3 inches from the cast-on edge, approximately 18 rounds.

4. Bind off loosely in pattern (see the "Binding Off in the Round" section in Chapter 2). Weave in yarn ends.

5. Wash and block, if desired.

Suggested Modifications

Once your project is complete, you may wish to embellish the surface with embroidery in contrasting colors of yarn. You can knit this pattern in various types of ribbing, or you might want to experiment with stitch patterns such as cables or knit-and-purl combinations (see Chapter 10 for some options).

Duplicate stitch

Who doesn't need a good potholder? Mine take a fair amount of abuse on a daily basis, dividing their time between protecting my hands and shielding my counter from hot pans. These handy kitchen accessories knit up fast. Make a whole pile of them to match your kitchen décor. With a little embellishment, they make excellent gifts. Using one skein each of the colors featured here, you can make all of the potholders pictured and still have yarn left over.

Potholder B

Potholder C

Potholder A

Specifications

SIZE
Finished dimensions: 9 inches × 9 inches

MATERIALS
115 yards of worsted-weight yarn: Lion Brand *LB Collection Organic Wool* (100% wool, 185 yd./ 3½ oz. skein)

Potholder A (worked in stockinette stitch): 1 skein in color Natural

Potholder B (worked in garter stitch): 1 skein in color Redwood

Potholder C (worked in stockinette stitch stripes): 1 skein each in colors Redwood, Avocado, Natural, and Dark Teal

NEEDLES
You can use any of the following needles in size US 8 (5mm), or size to obtain gauge:

One 16-inch circular needle

One set of 4 or 5 double-pointed needles

One 32- to 40-inch circular needle

Two 16-inch circular needles

NOTIONS
Stitch markers
Seaming needle

GAUGE
4 stitches per inch in stockinette, worked in the round

Plan the Potholder

CHOOSE A CIRCULAR KNITTING TECHNIQUE

You can work any of the potholders in this section with any of the four circular knitting techniques covered in Chapter 2. This project is so quick and easy that you may want to make four different potholders, each using a different technique.

CHOOSE YOUR YARN

It is very important with this project to use yarns that are 100-percent wool or cotton. Only these two fibers can be relied upon to protect you from the heat. An acrylic or acrylic-blend yarn will melt when exposed to high temperatures. Superwash wools are also not recommended for this project because the treatment the fiber undergoes to make it machine washable changes its characteristics significantly.

A good yarn choice for this project would be one that is rugged and durable; for these potholders, durability is more important than softness or comfort. Consider using a medium to dark color to help hide stains and spills because these potholders will see a great deal of use. Should your potholder find its way into the washing machine, do not fear! If you have made it out of 100-percent wool, it may return smaller and thicker, but the fulling that will have occurred (see the felted tote pattern in Chapter 7 for more information on fulling) will actually make it better at protecting you or your tabletop from the heat.

Make the Potholders

POTHOLDER A: STOCKINETTE STITCH

Follow the instructions here to create a stockinette-stitch potholder (Potholder A).

① Leaving an extra-long 24-inch tail, cast on 72 stitches with Natural and arrange your work on the needles according to the directions for your chosen knitting method (see Chapter 2). Join your work to knit in the round, being careful not to twist your cast on around the needles. Place a stitch marker to indicate the end of the round.

Potholder A

2 Knit 1 round.

3 Repeat Step 2 until your work measures about 9 inches from the cast-on edge.

4 Bind off loosely (see the "Bind Off in the Round" section in Chapter 2) and cut the yarn, leaving an extra-long 24-inch tail.

5 Using the extra-long yarn tails that you created during the cast on and bind off, seam each end of the potholder using a whipstitch (see Appendix).

6 Weave in the yarn ends.

Whipstitch edge

POTHOLDER B: GARTER STITCH

The potholder shown here was worked completely in garter stitch to increase its thickness. To make it, do the following:

1 Cast on with Redwood according to the directions above.

2 Knit 1 round, then purl 1 round.

3 Repeat Step 2 until your work measures 9 inches from the cast-on edge.

4 Bind off and finish as directed above.

NOTE: The extra thickness of this potholder will require more yarn to complete.

Potholder B

POTHOLDER C: STRIPED

Potholders are an excellent way to use up yarn scraps from other projects and experiment with changing colors. However, be sure that all of the yarn you use meets the criteria outlined in "Choose Your Yarn" on the previous page.

To make the striped potholder shown here, do the following:

Potholder C

① Cast on with Redwood according to the directions for Potholder A and knit for 6 rounds.

② Change to Avocado and knit for 6 rounds.

③ Change to Natural and knit for 6 rounds.

④ Change to Dark Teal and knit for 6 rounds.

⑤ Change back to Redwood and knit for 6 rounds.

⑥ Repeat steps 2–5 once.

⑦ Bind off and finish as directed for Potholder A above.

Suggested Modifications

A potholder would be a great project to experiment with stranded colorwork patterns (see Chapter 10 for some stitch pattern suggestions). You can also add a creative touch by crocheting a slip-stitch crochet edging as shown here, or whipstitching around the entire outside edge of the potholder with a contrasting color.

Fingerless Mitts

Another great way to practice working with the techniques outlined in Chapter 2 is to make a pair of fingerless mitts. Knit in a comfortable gauge of 4 stitches per inch, these will work up in no time at all. Make a pair to match the simple ear warmer presented earlier in this chapter, and you're fashionably set for cool-weather outings. If you would like to make both projects in the same yarn, you will need about 125 yards of worsted-weight yarn.

Specifications

SIZE
Finished dimensions: 6 inches in circumference (unstretched) $\times$ 7¼ inches long, to fit most adult hands

MATERIALS
80 yards of worsted-weight yarn: Peace Fleece Worsted (70% wool/30% mohair, 200 yd./4 oz. skein), 1 skein in color Glasnost Gold

NEEDLES
You can use any of the following needles in size US 8 (5mm), or size to obtain gauge:

One set of 4 or 5 double-pointed needles
One 32- to 40-inch circular needle
Two 16-inch circular needles

NOTIONS
Stitch markers
Seaming needle

GAUGE
4 stitches per inch in stockinette, worked in the round

Plan Your Mitts

CHOOSE A CIRCULAR KNITTING TECHNIQUE

You can work these mitts on double-pointed needles, with the magic loop method, or with two circulars. Because of their small circumference, they are not suitable for the traditional method of knitting with one circular. See Chapter 2 for more details on the various methods of knitting in the round.

CHOOSE YOUR YARN

A worsted-weight yarn that is both warm and soft would be a good choice for this project. Choose a fiber that has good elasticity because you want your mitts to stay on your hands comfortably and not stretch out and sag. See Chapter 5 for more information about choosing yarn.

Make the Mitts

1 Cast on 28 stitches and arrange your work on the needles according to the directions for your chosen knitting method (see Chapter 2). Join your work to knit in the round, being careful not to twist your cast on around the needles. Place a stitch marker to indicate the end of the round.

2 *Knit 3, purl 1. Repeat from * to the end of the round.

3 Repeat Step 2 until your work measures about 5 inches from the cast-on edge.

4 At the beginning of the next round, create a hole for your thumb (shown at right) as follows:

Bind off the next 4 stitches, then work in knit 3, purl 1 rib to the end of the round.

⑤ Using the backward-loop cast-on (see Appendix), create 4 new stitches at the beginning of the round. Then work in knit 3, purl 1 rib to the end of the round.

⑥ On the next round, work all stitches in the knit 3, purl 1 rib pattern. Work the first 4 stitches fairly tightly to prevent a gap from forming on either side of the new thumb hole.

⑦ Continue working in pattern as established until your work measures 2¼ inches from the edge of the thumb hole.

⑧ Bind off loosely in pattern (see the "Bind Off in the Round" section in Chapter 2). Weave in yarn ends.

⑨ Repeat steps 1–8 to make a second mitt to match.

⑩ Wash and block the mitts, if desired.

Suggested Modifications

Once your project is complete, you may wish to embellish the surface with embroidery in contrasting colors of yarn. You can knit this pattern in various types of ribbing, or you might want to experiment with stitch patterns such as cables or knit-and-purl combinations (see Chapter 10 for some options).

A different type of ribbing

CHAPTER 5

Planning a Project

Choosing a size, deciding on a yarn, choosing a stitch pattern (if you want one), and determining the gauge are all very important steps in the process of creating hand-knitted items. Additionally, some of the patterns in this book use the idea of a master pattern: a template of sorts into which you can insert your own yarn choices, sizes, and design ideas. The information presented in this chapter will allow you to adapt the master patterns to meet your design goals.

Choose a Size

One of the first steps in using the master patterns in this book is to choose a size. Deciding which size to knit is easy once you understand what and how to measure, as well as how ease affects the size of a finished garment.

Ease and Fit

Ease is the difference between the circumference of a finished garment and the size of the person who will wear it. *Positive ease* means that the unstretched circumference of the finished garment is larger than the circumference of the person who will wear it. A garment with positive ease fits loosely on the body—for example, a sweater worn over other clothing requires positive ease to fit properly.

Positive ease

Negative ease means the opposite; the unstretched circumference of the garment is smaller than the circumference of the person. A garment with negative ease stretches to fit snugly.

Negative ease is often desirable in garments worn close to the skin, such as form-fitting tank tops or other body-hugging styles of sweaters. When I knit a hat, however, I don't like it to be too snug, so I strive for not more than an inch of negative ease.

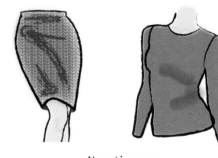

Negative ease

TIP

Socks should always have negative ease so that they are not baggy and uncomfortable to wear. I like my socks to be very snug and generally aim for 1 inch of negative ease in the finished project.

With regard to sweaters, ease is a matter of personal taste; however, some garments lend themselves to specific amounts of ease. If you are unsure about how much ease you should include, try measuring a similar garment already in your wardrobe that fits you well. Use that measurement when choosing the right size for you.

Measuring and Choosing a Size

After considering how loose or tight you would like your garment to be, it's time to measure the intended wearer to find their base measurement. For a sweater, measure the chest or bustline; for a sock, measure around the ball of the foot; for a hat, measure the circumference of the head, just above the ears.

Some patterns will also give you more detailed instructions about where and how to measure. You can use that measurement in conjunction with information contained in the pattern to determine the right size to knit.

Patterns state sizes based on the actual finished measurements of the garment. These measurements are given "unstretched," which means that you lay

Measure circumference of head just above ears

Measure the chest/bust at the widest point

the garment flat to measure it. You then use these numbers to determine which size to knit. For example, if you have a 36-inch chest and you are planning to make a loose sweater with 2 inches of positive ease, you should choose the size that has a finished circumference of about 38 inches. However, if you are making a tank top for which you want 1 inch of negative ease, you should choose the size that has a finished circumference of about 35 inches.

Select Yarn for a Project

Another important step in using master patterns or in making any of the projects in this book is yarn selection. You have many options from which to choose, and it is easy to feel overwhelmed. Knowing a little bit about yarn helps you make better choices when planning your knitting projects.

Fiber

ANIMAL FIBERS

Most yarn is made from the wool of sheep. Wool has excellent elasticity or bounce and tends to hold its shape well in a finished garment. It's also very warm. I think wool is good for just about any knitting project, particularly outerwear and socks.

Wool from different breeds of sheep can have different properties; some wools are very soft and springy, such as merino, while others are coarser. Wool can also be processed in different ways to emphasize certain desirable characteristics. Some wool yarns retain many of the properties of natural, untreated fleece, while others may be processed into super-soft yarns that most people would feel comfortable wearing against their skin. There are even machine-washable wool yarns available. Wool is, for me, the fiber of choice in most situations.

Mixed wool

Merino wool

Fibers from other animals—rabbits, goats, and alpacas, among many others—can be used to make yarn as well. Those yarns don't always bear the name of the animal whose fiber makes up the basis of the yarn. For example, angora comes from the undercoat of certain rabbit breeds. It is spun into yarn that is very soft, and when you wash and block it, the halo created by the angora fibers cannot be matched. It makes exceptionally warm sweaters and accessories or a luxurious trim.

Angora

Two very different fibers come from goats: mohair from angora goats and cashmere from cashmere goats. Mohair has little elasticity but is extremely durable. It feels a little scratchy to some people, but leaves a lovely, soft halo on the surface of your finished project. It is great for outerwear and accessories, and for socks when blended with other fibers. Cashmere, in stark contrast, is a very soft fiber that feels quite luxurious. Because it is such a soft and fine fiber, it is perfect for wearing against the skin or for use in accessories such as shawls.

Mohair   Cashmere

Alpaca yarn is made from the undercoat of the alpaca. Some alpaca yarns may still contain hairs, called *guard hairs*. These guard hairs are ideally removed before the yarn is spun, as they will shed from the yarn over time. Alpaca fibers are soft, warm, and dense, but they lack the elasticity of wool and the durability of mohair. Garments made solely from alpaca are not likely to hold their shape when finished. I tend to avoid alpaca yarn unless it is blended with some wool to give it more elasticity and durability.

NONANIMAL FIBERS

Yarn can also be made from nonanimal fibers, such as silk, cotton, linen, hemp, acrylic, and nylon. The list goes on, but this is a good representation of the wide range of nonanimal fibers that are available. These fibers have the benefit of being safe for people with animal fiber allergies or sensitivities, and they are mostly machine washable. However, always read and follow your yarn label advice when washing any yarn.

Silk

Silk comes from the cocoon of a particular type of moth. It is very soft and durable and excellent at retaining warmth. It can be difficult to work with because the fibers are very smooth and slippery and lack elasticity. However, it can also add drape and luster to a project.

Plant fibers such as cotton, linen, and hemp share some qualities. Most plant-based yarns are not as good at retaining body heat as natural animal fibers. This can be a benefit depending on where you plan on wearing your garment. They also lack elasticity but are quite strong. Cotton is very absorbent. It can be spun into yarn that enhances its natural softness, or it can be spun so that its strength and durability take center stage. Linen comes from the flax plant, and hemp from the hemp plant. Both of these fibers are quite crisp and even stiff, but they soften with repeated washing. Linen and hemp yarns are long-wearing and make garments suitable for warm weather.

Hemp

Linen   Cotton

Acrylic and nylon are man-made fibers. They are elastic, strong, and resistant to damage from insects. Nylon is often blended with natural fibers in small quantities to give it strength, as in many sock yarns. Acrylic is often used as a wool substitute for people with allergies, and is often found blended with wool.

The one type of yarn I have neglected to mention is novelty or "fashion" yarn. These yarns sometimes look like a string of Muppet fur or sometimes like an unraveled disco light. I love these yarns for their fun factor, but I've learned that they perform best as accents or in smaller accessories, not in whole garments. Also, I do not recommend these yarns for beginners. What looks like entertainment when it's in the skein can quickly become frustration when all that fluff or sparkle obscures your stitches.

Novelty yarns

Ease of Care

Washability is a big issue for some people and a minor one for others. You should wash most animal fibers and blends by hand. You usually hand-wash silk, while you generally machine-wash cotton, linen, and most acrylics. Some fibers are machine dryable as well.

Machine-washable wools are readily available, but the processing used to make them washable takes away some of the qualities knitters value in wool. However, the ease of care makes it a trade-off that most knitters are willing to live with. Minimally processed wool yarns make great outerwear because they retain a lot of the characteristics that they had when they were still on the sheep. Lanolin may remain in the fiber; it's great for helping the wool resist moisture. The fibers have not been brushed or combed as much as processed yarn, so they still retain the scales and crimp that make them wooly and warm. In general, the more processed a yarn is, the more of its natural character is lost.

Always read your ball-band information carefully to determine the care requirements for your yarn. Spending a great deal of time on a 100-percent wool garment for yourself only to have it shrink in the wash to the dimensions of a doll sweater is disastrous (unless you're the doll!). In general, consider machine-washable yarns for baby items or household goods like blankets or pillows. Hand-washable yarns are good for most adult sweaters and outerwear like mittens and hats.

Pilling

Pilling is the term used to describe the small balls of fiber that sometimes appear on the surface of knitted items. Abrasion causes the fiber to unravel or break, resulting in loose ends that form pills. In general, single-ply yarns tend to pill more than yarns made of multiple plies (see Chapter 1 for more information on ply). Without the other plies to help distribute the force of wear, the fibers break down more quickly. Also, tightly spun yarns tend to pill less than loosely spun ones, but they also tend to be less soft.

In general, softer yarns tend to develop a fuzzy, worn appearance relatively quickly, whereas more rugged yarns maintain their appearance longer. When in doubt, knit a swatch about 4 inches square and rub the surface vigorously to simulate wear. Watch to see how quickly the yarn looks worn or damaged, and make your decisions accordingly. You can even rub a single strand of a yarn still in the skein to get some idea of its durability. If it looks fuzzy and starts to pill after a few good rubs between your fingers, imagine what it will look like after a few wearings.

Weight and Drape

Drape is the word used to describe how a fabric hangs on the body. A drapey fabric is soft and flexible and closely conforms to curves; a fabric with less drape is more rigid and holds its own shape. The drape of a yarn has a lot to do with its thickness; fine yarns are drapey, but bulky yarns are not. In addition, a looser gauge will result in more drape and a tighter one in less drape.

Some projects, such as items worn close to the skin, call for a drapey fabric, while others, such as outerwear, require less drape. Choosing a level of drape is largely a matter of personal preference. The best way to determine the drape of a particular yarn is to create a large swatch and wash and block it to get a feel for how it will wear in a whole garment.

Drapey and nondrapey fabrics

FYI

The Craft Yarn Council of America (CYCA) has developed a system for determining the weight of yarn that ranges from 0 for lace yarns to 6 for super-bulky yarns. See www.craftyarncouncil.com/weight.html for more information.

Cost

Unless you are lucky enough to have an unlimited budget, cost will affect your yarn choices. I know it does mine! Yarns are now available in such a wide range of prices that everyone should be able to find a yarn that suits their budget.

For most of us, luxury fibers like cashmere, qiviut (from the musk ox), buffalo, and camel are yarns that knitters swoon over and buy sparingly as little indulgences. A skein or two of these yarns is enough to make an accessory such as a hat, lace scarf, or fingerless gloves, but the amounts necessary to make a sweater can run into the hundreds of dollars.

Qiviut

Buffalo   Cashmere

Choose yarns for your knitting projects that fit within your budget. Get to know the prices of yarns from catalogs, store visits, and online searches, and try not to let yourself fall so hard for a yarn you cannot afford that you can't imagine the garment knit in anything but.

Color

Color is an issue that sometimes confuses knitters. Yarns come not only in a vast range of colors but in different types as well, from solid, consistently dyed yarns to soft heathers, tweeds, marls, and variegated styles. Heathers incorporate gray or black to soften the tone and give texture to yarns. Tweeds contain little bits of color supplied by fibers added to the yarn as it is spun. Marls are yarns that are made of different-colored plies all twisted together. Self-striping yarns are dyed so that when you knit them, the colors align to form stripes. Variegated yarns combine different colors and hues in one yarn.

Heather   Tweed   Marl

Working with solid colors, heathers, tweeds, and marls is pretty straightforward. What you see in the skein is a lot like what you will get when you knit the garment. The same cannot be said of variegated and self-striping yarns. Self-striping yarns are excellent for small items such as socks, mittens, or infant garments. In projects of this size, their striping patterns are shown to best advantage. However, use caution when thinking about using these yarns in a large project, because the color repeats are not long enough to allow the stripes to carry across the body of a garment.

Self-striping yarn in a knitted hat

Variegated yarns can work for or against the knitter. A phenomenon called *pooling* can occur with these yarns, where colors stack up against each other and create pools of one color instead of the more blended image you may have had in mind.

In the skein, variegated yarns can look quite different from the finished knitted product. Sometimes even a swatch will not give you an accurate picture of what the finished garment will look like.

Pooled   *Not pooled*

Hand dyed and variegated yarns are beloved by many for the way colors play across a garment, but if pooling occurs in your work in a way that displeases you, try working with two balls of yarn, alternating them every other row or every two rows. This can help to break up the areas of pooled color.

You can take advantage of the "blank canvas" aspect of a master pattern to introduce stitch patterns into your project—cables, lace, colorwork, and knit-and-purl combinations. Chapter 10 gives a sampling of stitch patterns of each of these types, but there are many resources for finding stitch pattern ideas beyond the ones in this book.

Barbara Walker's *A Treasury of Knitting Patterns* (in four volumes), the *Vogue Knitting Stitchionary* series, and the *Harmony Guides* series are some of the many excellent resources available. I personally love Lesley Stanfield's book *The New Knitting Stitch Library*, but it may be hard to find.

Keep in mind that your gauge will change when using different patterns, so be sure to swatch in any stitch pattern you might want to use for your project. If you plan to include a cable, for example, make a swatch in the charted pattern. The same goes for lace, colorwork, or knit-and-purl combinations. Some patterns draw your work in more than others, and this is important to know as you move into measuring gauge. Make sure that you like the look and feel of a patterned swatch. If you are in doubt, make another swatch in a different yarn or stitch pattern—it's better to change your plan now on a small scale than to knit the whole garment and decide you don't like it (see the "Gauge and Swatching" section for more details on swatching).

Also make sure that the number of stitches to be cast on for your project is evenly divisible by the number of stitches in your chosen stitch pattern. Some master patterns (like the cowl pattern in Chapter 6) are very adjustable, but with more complicated patterns (such as the sock pattern in Chapter 7), it is important to stay with the stated number of cast-on stitches. Each master pattern gives information on how you can adapt it.

Gauge and Swatching

Beginning knitters often see swatching as a waste of time and yarn, while knitters with more experience tend to embrace the swatching process. This section helps you to understand why swatching is so important to increasing your satisfaction with the finished project.

What Is Gauge?

Gauge is critical to almost every knitting project. It is defined as the number of stitches horizontally and the number of rows vertically that occur in an inch of knitting. All patterns state an intended gauge. Even the master patterns in this book rely on gauge to determine the number of stitches you should cast on.

Most yarn labels give a recommended gauge. Some manufacturers express gauge in abbreviations like "8 sts = 1" on #1 needle." Some state both stitch and row gauge, as in "8 sts × 10 rows on US 1." That means the manufacturer feels that the yarn looks best when knit at about 8 stitches and 10 rows per inch, and that most knitters can expect to achieve that gauge using a US 1 needle.

The gauge might also be expressed in this way: "32 sts × 40 rows = 4" US 1." In that case, divide the total number of stitches by the total number of inches to get the number of stitches in 1 inch (32 ÷ 4 = 8 sts/inch). Repeat that process for the row gauge (40 ÷ 4 = 10 rows/inch). If the gauge is given only in centimeters, be aware that 10 cm = 4 inches; 2.5 cm = 1 inch.

The gauge is also sometimes expressed on the ball band as a square indicating rows and stitches. Outside of this square is information pertaining to the swatch: its size (usually 4 × 4 inches ≠ 10 × 10 centimeters) and the number of rows and stitches needed to fill that size space. Inside this box is the size of the needles used to get that gauge, often given in both US and metric sizes.

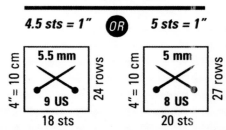

YARNS™	
Weight:	100 grams
Yardage:	247 yards
Gauge:	4 ½ sts = 1" on #8 needle or 5 sts = 1" on #7 needle

knitting gauges

4.5 sts = 1" **OR** 5 sts = 1"

4" = 10 cm | 5.5 mm ✕ 9 US | 24 rows
18 sts

4" = 10 cm | 5 mm ✕ 8 US | 27 rows
20 sts

Here's an aid to understanding gauge: Imagine building a wall with blocks. If your wall needs to measure a certain size when it is completed, you must base the dimensions of the wall on a certain size of block. If you use a different size block, the wall won't be the size you intended. So it is with your knitting. Each stitch acts as a block in the wall. If your stitches are too big, your project will also be too big. Make stitches too small and the reverse will happen.

The Importance of Swatching

You determine gauge by knitting a swatch and then measuring it to find out how many stitches and rows occur in an inch of knitted fabric. A swatch is simply a sample of knitting that you usually work in stockinette stitch or sometimes in the pattern stitch of the item you're planning to knit.

The needle size you personally need to get gauge can vary widely from that of other knitters. This has to do with each person's individual knitting style and the manner in which they hold and tension their yarn, among other variables. The needle size given on the ball band (or stated in your pattern) is a good starting point, but you should not assume that it will automatically give you the desired gauge. The only way to know is to knit a sample yourself.

*Swatches by 2 different knitters using same
yarn and same size needles*

Swatching is vital to ensure that your finished items fit properly. Many knitters in my classes complain about having to knit swatches until they learn to appreciate their importance (sometimes the hard way). Without a swatch to provide guidance and information about the yarn you're using and the needles you're knitting with, the project outcome may differ dramatically from what you intended. Given the amount of time and money you will invest in knitted projects, it is worth it to knit a proper swatch.

FAQ

Can I knit a swatch flat for an item I plan to knit in the round?

In general, the answer to that question is no. Although a purl is just the reverse side of a knit stitch, many knitters tend to work purl stitches a little looser than knit stitches. This phenomenon, called *rowing out*, can cause a difference in gauge between a project or swatch knit flat and one knit in the round. In order to accurately determine the gauge for your project, you should prepare your swatch in the same manner in which you intend to carry out the project.

Making a Swatch

There are two possible swatching scenarios. If you are following a pattern that specifies a gauge, you will need to make a swatch to match the gauge stated in the pattern. In this case, it is important that you match this number as closely as possible, especially when making fitted garments. On the other hand, if you are following a master pattern, you will need to swatch to find the gauge that you prefer for your chosen yarn. You have more freedom, but the gauge you choose must still be within the range presented by the master pattern. I outline both procedures here.

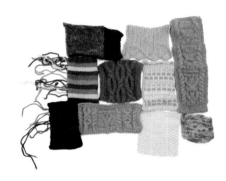

SWATCHING TO MATCH A STATED GAUGE

1 Decide on the size of your swatch. The minimum I recommend for a circular swatch is 6 inches in circumference and at least 4 inches in length. A swatch of that size will allow you to determine gauge by measuring a flat area in the center of the swatch (away from any edge distortion) that is about 2 inches wide and 2 inches long.

2 Once you have decided on the desired size of your swatch, determine the number of stitches to cast on to create that size swatch. Simply take the gauge given by the pattern (in stitches per inch) and multiply that number by the desired circumference of the swatch (in inches). For example, if a pattern specifies a gauge of 4 stitches per inch and you would like to make a swatch that is 6 inches in circumference, you would calculate the number of stitches to cast on as follows: 4 stitches/inch × 6 inches = 24 stitches to cast on.

Stitches to cast on = stitch gauge (in sts/inch) × desired circumference of swatch

3 Choose a needle size. You may have to change your needle size several times to be able to match the stated gauge. Start working with the needle size recommended in the pattern.

NOTE: When changing needle size for a swatch, you can estimate what size needles you might need by assuming that each needle size represents a difference of about ½ stitch per inch. This is a general rule and will not hold true for every knitter, but it's a good place to start.

④ Cast on the number of stitches that you calculated in Step 2 using one of the circular knitting methods described in Chapter 2. Then begin working in the round in the stitch pattern stated in the instructions for your project. This is usually stockinette, but the gauge could be given in a cable or lace pattern, so check the stated gauge carefully.

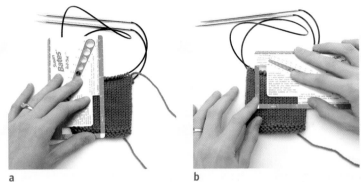

a   b

⑤ Continue to work in the round until your swatch measures about 4 inches from the cast-on edge (a). Then determine your stitch gauge, following the instructions in the "Measuring Gauge" section at the end of this chapter (b). If your measured stitch gauge is ½ stitch or more off from the specified gauge, make another swatch. Work the new swatch with a smaller needle if your gauge is less than the specified gauge; work it with a larger needle if your gauge is greater than the specified gauge.

NOTE: If your gauge is off by 1 whole stitch or more, consider using a needle that is 2 sizes smaller or larger.

⑥ Bind off your swatch and save it as a record of your work, or rip it out and cast on for your project.

NOTE: Some knitters save their swatches and project notes in a knitting notebook. This allows them to refer to information such as what yarn they used, or any modifications they made to the pattern.

TIP

The longer you knit, the more familiar you will become with your own personal knitting style. I knit loosely, which means that I need to use a needle 2 or 3 sizes smaller than the one recommended. Once you know what kind of knitter you are in terms of tension and gauge, you can choose a needle size that reflects that, which can save time in swatching. However, never assume that you will "get gauge." If you don't make a swatch, you're taking a big chance with your work.

Gauge and Swatching *(continued)*

SWATCHING FOR A MASTER PATTERN

1. Decide on the size of your swatch. The minimum I recommend for a circular swatch is 6 inches in circumference and 4 inches in length. A swatch of that size will allow you to determine gauge by measuring a flat area in the center of the swatch (away from any edge distortion) that is 2 inches wide and 2 inches long.

2. Determine the number of stitches to cast on to create your swatch. Take the gauge recommended on the ball band of your yarn (in stitches per inch) and multiply that number by the desired circumference of the swatch (in inches).

> **Stitches to cast on = stitch gauge (in sts/inch) × desired circumference of swatch**

If you will be using a stitch pattern for your project, modify this number so that it is a multiple of the number of stitches in one repeat of your chosen stitch pattern. Also, be sure to include enough repeats of the stitch pattern so that you will be able to measure gauge over at least one or two complete repeats on one side of the circular swatch. For example, if the ball band specifies a gauge of 5 stitches per inch and you would like to make a swatch that is 6 inches in circumference, you would calculate the number of stitches to cast on as follows: 5 stitches/inch × 6 inches = 30 stitches to cast on. If your chosen stitch pattern has a repeat of 4 stitches, cast on 32 stitches because that is the closest multiple of 4. That will give you 8 repeats of your stitch pattern, 4 on each side.

> **Number of repeats in swatch = stitches to cast on / nbr of sts in repeat**

3. Choose a needle size. You may have to change your needle several times to find the right size for your yarn and chosen stitch pattern. Start working with the needle size recommended on the ball band of your yarn.

4. Cast on the number of stitches that you calculated in Step 2 using one of the circular knitting methods described in Chapter 2. Then begin working in the round in the stitch pattern you have chosen for your project.

5 Continue to work in the round until your swatch measures at least 4 inches from the cast-on edge. Then assess your work. Do you like the stitch definition and the appearance and feel of the swatch? If you are making socks, you may want a dense fabric that will stand up to wear; if you are making a cowl, you may want a fabric with more drape. The master pattern will give suggestions about yarn selection that will help you decide what sort of appearance and texture you want to create.

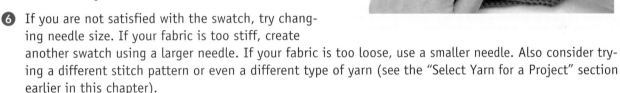

6 If you are not satisfied with the swatch, try changing needle size. If your fabric is too stiff, create another swatch using a larger needle. If your fabric is too loose, use a smaller needle. Also consider trying a different stitch pattern or even a different type of yarn (see the "Select Yarn for a Project" section earlier in this chapter).

It may take you several tries to get the fabric you want, but it is better to spend extra time swatching than to end up with a floppy mitten that lets the wind through or a cowl that is so stiff that it stands up by itself.

7 Once you have the look and feel you want, continue working until the swatch is at least 6 inches long. Then bind off your work, measure your gauge as explained in the "Measuring Gauge" section, on the following page, and record this information for use in the master pattern.

TIP

Instead of beginning a new swatch each time I change needles, I work my swatches as a long tube. I work one complete purl round when I change needles to clearly separate the sections knit with different needles. On the next round I make a series of yarnover buttonholes to indicate the needle size I am using. For example, if I am using US 6 needles, I make a series of six holes by working (yo, k2tog) six times total. The six holes are a record of the needle size within the work. This method works for needles that are "whole" sizes, but will not be effective for US sizes such as 1.5, 2.5, or 10.5.

Measuring Gauge

Assessing your swatches to determine your gauge is not complicated, but it is important to do it properly to get an accurate result.

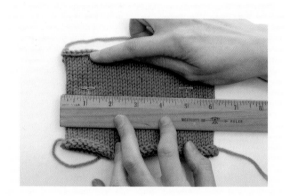

1 Lay your swatch out in front of you on a table or other smooth, flat surface. If your work is still on the needles, slip it onto a piece of waste yarn or onto the cable of a long circular needle so that the stitches are not compressed.

NOTE: To obtain the most accurate assessment of your gauge, it is best to wash and lightly block your swatch prior to measuring gauge. However, doing so is not always convenient. If you do have the time, it's a good idea to wash your swatch the same way you intend to wash the finished project. This will give a better indication of how the fabric will behave when you have knitted it up.

2 Using a ruler, place T-pins or straight pins into the swatch 4 inches apart from side to side. If your swatch does not allow you to pin a full 4 inches in width, then pin an area as wide as you can, but not less than 2 inches. Remember to stay away from the edges of the swatch where the stitches may be distorted. Record the width of this pinned area on a piece of paper.

FYI The ideal swatch measures at least 5 inches wide × 6 inches long. That allows you to determine gauge over a 4-inch-square section in the center of the swatch, away from any distortions that can occur at the edges of the work. When knitting a swatch in the round, it is only possible to measure half of the circumference at any one time (without cutting open the cylindrical swatch). Therefore, in order to achieve the ideal swatch circularly, you would have to create a swatch with a circumference of 10 inches. That said, the ideal swatch may not be the swatch you choose to knit for your project. A swatch that large is practically a project in itself.

③ Count the number of stitches that occur across one row between the pins. Be sure to include half or quarter stitches. Record this number of stitches on your paper. Then divide the number of stitches by the horizontal distance between the pins. This will give you your stitches per inch (or stitch gauge).

④ Reposition the pins so that they are 4 inches apart vertically along a column of stitches in the middle of your swatch. Then count the number of rows that occur in that column of stitches between the pins. Divide this number of rows by the vertical distance between the pins. This will give you your rows per inch (or row gauge).

NOTE: It is best to check your gauge in multiple areas of your swatch to be sure that your gauge is consistent.

TIP

Measuring gauge on a patterned swatch can be a little more difficult than measuring gauge in stockinette stitch. You may find it easier to pin off a certain number of repeats of the stitch pattern and then measure the distance between the pins. You can then calculate your stitch gauge by multiplying the number of stitches in each repeat by the number of repeats between the pins, and dividing that value by the horizontal distance between the pins. For example, if you marked off 2 repeats of your 9-stitch-wide stitch pattern and it measures 3 inches, your stitch gauge is 6 stitches per inch (2 × 9 stitches / 3 inches).

CHAPTER 6

Simple Projects

The projects in this chapter will enable you to test your new circular knitting skills. All three projects are presented as master patterns, allowing you to choose what size to knit and which weight and type of yarn you'd like to use. In all three patterns, I give suggestions for the type of needles best suited for the project: double-pointed needles, a shorter circular for the traditional method, a long circular for magic loop, or two circulars for the two-circular method. The choice is yours.

Simple Circular Cowl

This simple project, presented here as a master pattern, is the perfect starting point for knitting in the round. Choose the desired circumference of your cowl, make a gauge swatch to determine your cast-on number, and away you go! You can knit this cowl in plain stockinette stitch and allow it to curl at the edges, or add a simple border of garter stitch to control the natural roll of stockinette stitch. You can also knit it in a variety of stitch patterns; it lends itself well to lacy, open designs.

Cowl A   Cowl B   Cowl C

SIZE

XS (S, M, L, XL)

Circumference: 20 (26, 32, 44, 50) inches

This cowl is circular in shape. You can make it any circumference and height you want. The circumference is determined by the number of stitches you cast on; the height is determined by how many rounds you knit before you bind off. The L and XL sizes are intended to be wrapped twice around your neck.

Yardage for 20–50" Cowl That Is Approximately 12" Tall	
Gauge in Stockinette	**Approximate Yardage**
3 sts/inch	120–450 yards
4 sts/inch	160–500 yards
5 sts/inch	200–650 yards
6 sts/inch	260–800 yards
7 sts/inch	325–950 yards

YARN

You can use virtually any weight of yarn for this project. See the "Choose Your Yarn" section on page 127 for recommendations. The number of yards you need will vary, depending on gauge, stitch pattern, and the size of the cowl. The table (above, right) gives you a rough estimate.

Cowl A: Valley Yarns *Northfield* (70% merino/20% baby alpaca/10% silk, 124 yd. per ball), 3 balls in color Spice. This cowl was knit in stockinette stitch at a gauge of 5 stitches per inch on a US 6 needle. It has a circumference of 24 inches and is 12½ inches high.

Cowl B: Blue Moon Fiber Arts *Geisha* (70% kid mohair/20% mulberry silk/10% nylon, 995 yd. per skein), 1 skein in color Mochaberry. This cowl was knit in a lace pattern at a gauge of 4 stitches per inch on a US 5 needle. It has a circumference of 21 inches and is 16 inches high.

Cowl C: Buffalo Gold *Moon* (25% bison down/75% Tencel, 170 yd. per skein), 2 skeins in color Smoke. This cowl was knit in a lacy cable pattern at a gauge of 6 stitches per inch on a US 5 needle. It has a circumference of 20 inches and is 18 inches high.

NEEDLES

One 16-inch (or longer) circular needle in the size needed to get your desired gauge.

NOTIONS

Stitch markers
Seaming needle

Stitch Patterns

Lace Chart and Key for Cowl B (Multiple of 14 Stitches)

Key

Ⓠ	**Ktbl**: Knit I stitch through the back loop
☐	**K**: Knit
◩	Knit 4 stitches together as one
Ⓞ	**Yo**: Yarn over
◪	Slip I stitch as if to knit, k3tog, pass the slipped stitch over the k3tog

NOTE: If you plan to use this stitch pattern on your cowl, be sure to cast on a number of stitches that is a multiple of 14.

CABLE AND LACE CHART AND KEY FOR COWL C (MULTIPLE OF 17 STITCHES)

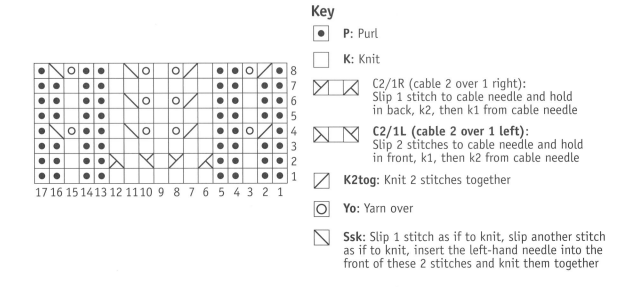

Key

●	**P:** Purl	
☐	**K:** Knit	
⌐⌐	**C2/1R (cable 2 over 1 right):** Slip 1 stitch to cable needle and hold in back, k2, then k1 from cable needle	
⌐⌐	**C2/1L (cable 2 over 1 left):** Slip 2 stitches to cable needle and hold in front, k1, then k2 from cable needle	
╱	**K2tog:** Knit 2 stitches together	
○	**Yo:** Yarn over	
╲	**Ssk:** Slip 1 stitch as if to knit, slip another stitch as if to knit, insert the left-hand needle into the front of these 2 stitches and knit them together	

NOTE: If you plan to use this stitch pattern on your cowl, be sure to cast on a number of stitches that is a multiple of 17.

Plan the Cowl

CHOOSE A CIRCULAR KNITTING METHOD

It is best to work this project using one circular needle in the traditional method. You can work smaller cowls on a 16-inch circular; larger cowls will fit better on a 32-inch circular. However, if you do not have the correct length of circular needle to fit all of your cast-on stitches, you can use two circulars or the magic loop method (see Chapter 2 for details). I do not recommend using double-pointed needles for this project due to the potentially large number of stitches.

CHOOSE A SIZE

Drape a tape measure or a 50-inch piece of string around your neck and arrange it to find your desired cowl circumference (a). This master pattern offers sizes ranging from 20 inches all the way up to 50 inches. The smaller cowls will fit once around your neck, and, if you knit it to a sufficient height, you can pull it up over the head as a snood (b).

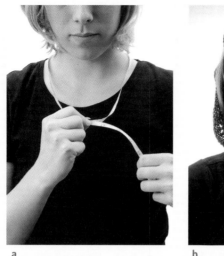

a

b

The 32-inch cowl can drape gracefully around the neck as both a fashion accessory and a buffer against the cold winter winds. The two largest sizes are large enough that you can wrap them twice around the neck for added warmth, or once around the neck as a dramatic accent.

CHOOSE YOUR YARN

When choosing yarn for your cowl, consider the purpose you want your finished project to fulfill. If you are seeking a year-round accessory, choose a yarn that reflects that; cotton, rayon, or silk would be comfortable just about anywhere. If you want a cowl item that's suited for cool-weather wear, try wool or another animal fiber. Think about color as well; a simple stockinette cowl will show the colors of a variegated or self-patterning yarn to best advantage, while a solid or semi-solid color yarn is more appropriate for a complicated stitch pattern.

CHOOSE A STITCH PATTERN AND DETERMINE YOUR GAUGE

After choosing your yarn, consider a stitch pattern. You can work this cowl in stockinette stitch, one of the lacy patterns presented in Cowl B or C, a stitch pattern from Chapter 10, or a pattern of your own. Once you've chosen a stitch pattern, make a swatch in that pattern to determine your gauge and your needle size. (See page 114 for details on swatching and measuring gauge.) Your gauge will determine the number of stitches you will cast on to achieve a given size. Bear in mind that your total number of cast-on stitches should be divisible by the number of stitches in your stitch pattern. For example, if your stitch pattern is 12 stitches wide, round the cast-on number from the table on the next page to a multiple of 12.

Make the Cowl

1 Using the long-tail cast-on (see page 28), cast on the number of stitches specified in the table at right for your gauge and desired cowl size.

2 Arrange your stitches on the needle and join for working in the round, being careful not to twist the cast-on around the needles. Place a marker to indicate the end of the round.

Cast-On for Cowl	
Gauge	Number of Stitches to Cast On
3 sts/inch	60 (78, 96, 132, 150)
4 sts/inch	80 (104, 128, 176, 200)
5 sts/inch	100 (130, 160, 220, 250)
6 sts/inch	120 (156, 192, 264, 300)
7 sts/inch	140 (182, 224, 308, 350)

3 If you want an edging, work a few rounds of garter stitch as follows: *Knit 1 round; purl 1 round. Repeat from * once.

4 Begin to work in stockinette or your chosen stitch pattern until the cowl measures the desired height from the cast-on edge.

NOTE: I recommend 12–24 inches for a single-wrap cowl and 8–12 inches for a longer cowl. The cowl should be at least 18 inches tall if you want to wear it as a snood.

5 If you want an edging, work a few rounds of garter stitch as follows: *Knit 1 round; purl 1 round. Repeat from * once.

6 Bind off loosely. Weave in yarn ends.

7 Wash and block, if desired. If you chose a lace pattern, it is especially important to block your finished item to open up the lace.

Cowl A

Cowl B

Cowl C

Using the master pattern below, this hat knits up very quickly and makes a great small gift. It has a paper-bag top that requires no decreasing. Simply knit the tube as long as you want, bind off, and close the top of the hat with a simple tie. This quick project is a great way to practice the techniques outlined in Chapter 2.

Child Hat A

Child Hat B

Specifications

SIZE

Child's S (M, L)

Brim circumference: 16 (18, 20) inches

YARN

Desired yarn in the amount specified.

Approximate Yardages for 16–20" Hat	
Gauge in Stockinette	Approximate Yardage
3 sts/inch	60–90 yards
4 sts/inch	85–125 yards
5 sts/inch	100–160 yards
6 sts/inch	135–225 yards
7 sts/inch	165–250 yards

NOTE: The estimates above are for a hat with a ribbed brim. The hemmed and rolled brims require slightly more yardage.

Hat A: Schaefer Yarns *Chris* (80% extra-fine merino wool superwash/20% nylon, 215 yd. per skein), 1 skein in color Julia Morgan. This hat, knit in size M, was worked at a gauge of 5 stitches per inch on a US 5 needle.

Hat B: Valley Yarns *Valley Superwash* (100% extra-fine merino superwash, 97 yd. per skein), 1 skein in color Blue Mist. This hat, knit in size S, was worked at a gauge of 5 stitches per inch on a US 5 needle.

NEEDLES

You can use any one of the following needles in the size needed to obtain your desired gauge:

    One 16-inch circular needle
    One set of 4 or 5 double-pointed needles
    One 32- to 40-inch circular needle
    Two 16-inch circular needles

NOTE: If you are working a rolled stockinette brim, you will need another needle of the same type, one size smaller than that used to obtain your desired gauge.

NOTIONS

Stitch marker
Seaming needle

Plan Your Hat

CHOOSE A CIRCULAR KNITTING METHOD

You can work this project using any of the circular knitting methods described in Chapter 2. However, the smallest size may be difficult to work on a 16-inch circular because the stitches may be stretched out along the needle. I prefer to knit small hats using the magic-loop method with one long circular needle.

CHOOSE A HAT SIZE

Determine the desired circumference for the hat. Most hats should be knit with negative ease (see page 104 for details about ease). Measure around the widest part of the intended wearer's head and subtract $\frac{1}{2}$–$1\frac{1}{2}$ inches from that measurement to calculate the hat circumference.

NOTE: A hemmed brim is not as stretchy as a rolled or ribbed brim, so it's best not to include too much negative ease when using this hem.

CHOOSE YOUR YARN

Choose a yarn that is both machine washable and soft against the skin. Superwash yarns save moms some work, and softer yarns make hats that kids will wear. If a child has allergies or sensitivities to animal fiber, choose a cotton or acrylic yarn that meets the criteria above. If the hat will be worn in colder weather, I tend to stick with heavier yarns: bulky, worsted, or DK weight. I like to match the colors of hats and mittens for children with their current outerwear. Because this project is so simple to knit with very little patterning, it's a great place to use a variegated or self-patterning yarn.

DETERMINE YOUR GAUGE

After choosing your yarn, make a swatch in stockinette to determine your gauge and needle size. See "Swatching for a Master Pattern" on page 118 for details on swatching and measuring gauge.

Make the Hat

① Using the long-tail cast-on (see page 28), cast on the number of stitches specified in the table below for your gauge and desired hat size.

Cast-On for Hat	
Gauge	**Number of Stitches to Cast On**
3 sts/inch	48 (54, 60)
4 sts/inch	64 (72, 80)
5 sts/inch	80 (90, 100)
6 sts/inch	96 (108, 120)
7 sts/inch	112 (126, 140)

② Arrange your stitches on the needles according to your chosen circular knitting method (see Chapter 2). Join for working in the round, being careful not to twist the cast-on around the needles. Place a marker to indicate the end of the round.

BRIM

Follow the directions below for the brim style you want.

Ribbed Brim

① *Knit 1, purl 1; repeat from * to beginning of round.

NOTE: Other rib patterns that are good for the bottom of a hat are 2 × 2, 2 × 1, and 3 × 1. Remember that your chosen rib pattern must fit evenly into your number of cast-on stitches.

② Continue working in rib for 1½ inches or the desired length from the cast-on edge.

③ Go to the "Body" section on the next page.

ROLLED STOCKINETTE BRIM

1. Using a needle one size smaller than the one you will use for the body of your hat, knit for 2 inches.

2. Change back to the larger needle and work the remainder of the hat as specified in the "Body" section below.

HEMMED BRIM

1. Work in stockinette stitch until the hat measures 1 inch from the cast-on edge.

2. Purl 1 round to create a turning ridge.

3. Work 1 more inch of stockinette stitch.

4. Go to the "Body" section below to work the remainder of the hat.

NOTE: See photo of Adult Hat A on page 136 for an example of a hemmed brim.

BODY

1. Work in stockinette stitch until the hat measures 6½ (7, 7½) inches from the edge of the brim. If using a hemmed brim, measure from the purled turning round. If using a rolled brim, measure from the bottom of the rolled brim. If using a ribbed brim, measure from the cast-on edge.

2. Bind off loosely. Weave in yarn ends.

3. If you worked a hemmed brim, fold the bottom edge up inside the hat along the purled turning round. Loosely whipstitch the hem in place on the wrong side (see Appendix).

4. Cut two or three strands of yarn about 12 inches long. Holding these strands together, tie them tightly around the top of the hat about 1½ inches from the bound-off edge. Using a seaming needle, take the yarn ends to the inside and weave them in.

Hats for Grown-ups

This hat is similar to the children's version, but I have added directions for shaping the top. There are three options for the brim. You can work this hat in plain stockinette stitch in a colorful or fashion yarn, or you can customize it by working the colorwork pattern shown here. Don't feel tied to those two options, however. You can use this hat as a canvas to express yourself. Try a stitch pattern from Chapter 10 or another pattern that appeals to you.

Adult Hat A

Adult Hat B

Specifications

SIZE
Adult's S (M, L)

Brim circumference: 20 (21, 22) inches

YARN
Desired yarn in the amount specified in the table below.

Approximate Yardages for 20–22" Hat	
Gauge in Stockinette	Approximate Yardage
3 sts/inch	80–100 yards
4 sts/inch	110–140 yards
5 sts/inch	140–180 yards
6 sts/inch	180–225 yards
7 sts/inch	220–275 yards

NOTE: The estimates above are for a hat with a ribbed brim. The hemmed and rolled brims require slightly more yardage.

Hat A: Foxfire Fiber *Upland Wool & Alpaca* (80% wool/20% prime alpaca, 135 yd. per skein), 1 skein in color Moss. This hat, knit in size S, was worked at a gauge of 4 stitches per inch on a US 6 needle.

Hat B: Valley Yarns *Berkshire* (85% wool/15% alpaca, 141 yd. per skein), 1 skein each in colors (A) Dark Brown, (B) Pale Lilac, and (C) Stone Blue. This hat, knit in size S, was worked at a gauge of 4 stitches per inch on a US 6 needle.

NEEDLES

One of the following types of needles in the size needed to obtain your desired gauge:

> One set of 4 or 5 double-pointed needles
>
> One 32- to 40-inch circular needle
>
> Two 16-inch circular needles
>
> One 16-inch circular needle and a set of double-pointed needles for working the crown decreases

NOTE: If you are working a rolled stockinette brim, you will need another needle of the same type, one size smaller than that used to obtain your desired gauge.

NOTIONS

Stitch markers

Seaming needle

Stitch Pattern

COLORWORK CHART FOR HAT B (MULTIPLE OF 5 STITCHES)

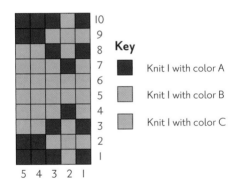

Key

Knit I with color A

Knit I with color B

Knit I with color C

NOTE: If you plan to use this stitch pattern on your hat, be sure to cast on a number of stitches that is a multiple of 5.

Plan Your Hat

CHOOSE A CIRCULAR KNITTING METHOD

You can work this project using any of the circular knitting methods described in Chapter 2. If you knit the hat on one 16-inch circular needle, you will need to switch to double-pointed needles (or one of the other methods) at some point during the crown decreases because the stitches will no longer reach comfortably around the needle. I prefer to knit hats using the magic-loop method with one long circular needle.

CHOOSE A SIZE

Determine the circumference you want for the hat. Most hats should be knit with negative ease (see page 104 for details about ease). Measure around the widest part of the intended wearer's head (see photo on page 130) and subtract ½–1½ inches from that measurement to calculate the hat circumference.

NOTE: A hemmed brim is not as stretchy as a rolled or ribbed brim, so it's best not to include too much negative ease when using this hem.

CHOOSE YOUR YARN

Yarn for adult hats can run the gamut from practical to frivolous and fun. If I want a warm winter hat, for example, I will choose a yarn that is warm and durable, and I will knit it at a tighter gauge than recommended on the ball band. This results in a denser fabric that better retains heat. I will also choose a 100-percent wool yarn that's been processed as little as possible. If, on the other hand, I am creating a fun accessory, I might choose a fashion yarn that adds a little flair. Because this hat is such a simple shape, it's a great way to show off variegated or self-striping yarns.

DETERMINE YOUR GAUGE

After choosing your yarn, make a swatch in stockinette to determine your gauge and needle size. (See page 114 for details on swatching and measuring gauge.)

Make the Hat

CAST ON

1 Using the long-tail cast-on (see page 28), cast on the number of stitches specified in the table at right for your gauge and desired hat size.

2 Arrange your stitches on the needles according to your chosen circular knitting method (see Chapter 2). Join for working in the round, being careful not to twist the cast-on around the needles. Place a marker to indicate the end of the round.

Cast-On for Hat	
Gauge	Number of Stitches to Cast On
3 sts/inch	60 (64, 66)
4 sts/inch	80 (84, 88)
5 sts/inch	100 (104, 110)
6 sts/inch	120 (128, 132)
7 sts/inch	140 (146, 154)

BRIM
Follow the directions below for the desired brim style.

RIBBED BRIM
1 *Knit 1, purl 1; repeat from * to beginning of round.

NOTE: Other rib patterns that are good for the bottom of a hat are 2 × 2, 2 × 1, and 3 × 1. Remember that your chosen rib pattern must fit evenly into your number of cast-on stitches.

2 Continue working in rib for 2 inches or the desired length from the cast-on edge.

3 Go to the "Body" section on the next page.

Ribbed brim and colorwork of Adult Hat B

ROLLED STOCKINETTE BRIM
1 Using a needle one size smaller than the one you will use for the body of your hat, knit for 2 inches.

2 Change back to the larger needle and work the remainder of the hat as specified in the "Body" section below.

HEMMED BRIM
1 Work in stockinette stitch until the hat measures 1 inch from the cast-on edge.

2 Purl 1 round to create a turning ridge.

3 Work 1 more inch of stockinette stitch.

4 Go to the "Body" section below to work the remainder of the hat.

Hemmed brim of Adult Hat A

BODY
1 Begin to work the body of the hat in stockinette stitch or the desired stitch pattern.

NOTE: To use the colorwork pattern shown in Hat B, work 1 round of stockinette in the main color before beginning the chart. See page 85 for tips about working with color in the round.

2 Continue in pattern until the hat measures 5½ (6, 6½) inches from the edge of the brim, or 3¼ (3½, 3¾) inches less than total desired length.

NOTE: If using a hemmed brim, measure from the purled turning round. If using a rolled brim, measure from the bottom of the rolled brim. If using a ribbed brim, measure from the cast-on edge.

TOP SHAPING

1 Setup Round: Decrease the number of stitches on your needles to the nearest multiple of 8 by working the number of decreases specified in the table below, evenly spaced around the circumference of the hat.

NOTE: If the table indicates zero stitches to decrease, just work a plain stockinette round.

Number of Stitches to Decrease on Setup Round		
Gauge	To Decrease	Remaining
3 sts/inch	4 (0, 2)	56 (64, 64)
4 sts/inch	0 (4, 0)	80 (80, 88)
5 sts/inch	4 (0, 6)	96 (104, 104)
6 sts/inch	0 (0, 4)	120 (128, 128)
7 sts/inch	4 (2, 2)	136 (144, 152)

2 Knit 1 round, placing a marker after each set of stitches (as indicated in the table below).

Location of Decrease Markers	
Gauge	Number of Stitches between Markers
3 sts/inch	7 (8 ,8)
4 sts/inch	10 (10, 11)
5 sts/inch	12 (13, 13)
6 sts/inch	15 (16, 16)
7 sts/inch	17 (18, 19)

6 Cut the yarn, leaving a 10-inch tail. Thread this tail onto a seaming needle and pull the needle through the remaining 8 stitches. Pull snugly to close.

7 Weave in yarn ends.

8 If you worked a hemmed brim, fold the bottom edge up inside the hat along the purled turning round. Loosely whipstitch the hem in place on the wrong side (see Appendix).

3 *Knit to 2 stitches before the marker, k2tog; repeat from * to the end of the round.

4 Knit 1 round.

5 Repeat steps 3 and 4 until 8 stitches remain.

NOTE: If you are working the hat on one 16-inch circular needle, change to double-pointed needles (or one of the other circular knitting methods) when your stitches no longer fit comfortably around your needle.

TIP

There are a lot of ways to customize this hat. For a stocking cap, work 2 to 4 plain knit rounds between decrease rounds while decreasing the top. Top the hat with a pompom, tassel, or little I-cord braid. You can also experiment with cables, knit-and-purl combinations, stripes, or stranded colorwork. See Chapter 10 for some stitch patterns to try.

CHAPTER 7

Intermediate Projects

Now that you've warmed up, presumably, on the projects featured in the previous chapters, it's time to cut your teeth on some projects that require a little more shaping. Beginning with a felted tote bag, then mittens, and then socks, this chapter takes the skills you've already learned and adds a little curve, literally!

Felted Tote Bag

I love bags, and I love making them, too. This simple felted tote is a great way to use up remnants of bulky yarn—just be sure that the yarn is wool.

Felting is an inexact science; different wool yarns felt at different rates. Your finished bag may not have exactly the same dimensions as the samples shown here, but the result will still be a useful, cute tote that you made yourself. Because felting makes knitted fabric sturdier and less penetrable, this project makes an excellent market tote or knitting bag.

Felted Tote Bag A

Felted Tote Bag B

Specifications

SIZE
Finished bag: approximately 13 inches × 16 inches

YARN
About 365 yards of bulky-weight yarn

Tote Bag A: Schaefer Yarn *Esperanza* (70% lambs-wool/30% alpaca, 280 yd. per skein), 2 skeins of color (A) Nellie Bly

Tote Bag B: Valley Yarns *Northampton Bulky* (100% wool, 109 yd. per skein), 3 skeins of color (A) Raspberry Heather and 1 skein of color (B) Chocolate

NEEDLES
You can use either of the following needles in size US 11, or size needed to obtain gauge:

Two 16-inch (or longer) circular needles
One 40-inch circular needle

NOTE: See "Choose a Circular Knitting Method" on the next page for details on choosing needles.

NOTIONS
Stitch markers
Seaming needle
Sharp pair of scissors (for cutting bag after felting)

GAUGE
About 2½ to 3 stitches per inch in stockinette stitch *before felting*. (Matching stitch gauge is not critical for this project. The size of the finished bag will vary depending on the yarn used.)

Plan Your Bag

CONSTRUCTION OVERVIEW

Although the term *felting* refers to any material in which wool fibers are matted together into a denser fabric, this project is more correctly referred to as *fulled*. *Fulling* applies to items that you first knit and then reduce in size by applying heat, water, and agitation.

You work this tote bag from the bottom up. You cast on stitches using a special technique that creates a closed bottom, and then use increases to shape the bottom of the bag. Later, you work decreases to give the sides a vase-like shape. After you bind off the top of the bag and run the ends in, you full (or felt) the bag until it is reduced to the size you want. You then cut handles directly into the felted material, and lay the bag flat to dry.

NOTE: Be aware as you knit this bag that it will be significantly larger than you expect until after it has been felted.

CHOOSE A CIRCULAR KNITTING METHOD

You can cast on and work the bottom of this bag using either two circular needles (of any length) or one 40-inch circular in the magic-loop method (see Chapter 2 for details on these techniques). If desired, you can switch to one 16-inch or 24-inch circular needle once you have worked enough increases that the stitches will fit comfortably around the needle. I do not recommend using double-pointed needles for this project.

CHOOSE YOUR YARN

This project requires specific yarn. The best choice is a 100-percent wool yarn. At a minimum, the yarn should contain not less than 75-percent wool. Yarns that do not contain at least 75-percent wool will generally not felt because they lack wool's special properties that make it felt together when exposed to heat and agitation. You may choose a bulky yarn for which the label specifies 3–3½ stitches per inch. It might also be possible to work with two strands of worsted-weight yarn held together.

MAKE A SWATCH AND FELT IT

With this tote, swatching is critical. Follow the directions below to make a swatch in your desired yarn and then check its gauge both before and after felting.

① Using your chosen yarn and needles, cast on 18 stitches. Do not join; you will work this swatch flat.

② Work 20 rows of stockinette. Then bind off loosely and weave in yarn ends.

3 Measure your swatch and record its total width and height. The swatches made for the bags pictured here measured approximately 6½ inches wide × 5¾ inches tall before felting. If your swatch is roughly the same size, proceed to the next step. If your swatch is appreciably larger, create another swatch using a smaller needle(s). If your swatch is much smaller, create another swatch using a larger needle(s).

4 Felt your swatch by following the directions in the "Finishing" section on page 144.

5 After felting, measure your swatch again. The swatches made for the bags pictured here measured approximately 5 inches wide × 3½ inches tall after felting. If your swatch is roughly the same size, proceed with the instructions to make the bag. If your swatch is much larger, try felting the swatch again to see if it will shrink further. If your swatch is much smaller, make another swatch using larger needles, consider changing yarns, or be aware that your finished bag will be smaller than the bags shown.

NOTE: During felting, the bag loses much more height than width. This is true of all felted projects.

Make the Bag

NOTE: In this pattern, I worked every make 1 increase as a backward-loop make 1 (see page 233). You can use another increase if you prefer.

BOTTOM OF BAG

① Using color A and the figure-8 cast-on (see page 235), cast on 44 stitches. Divide so that there are 22 on each of two circular needles or on each end of one long circular needle. Each set of 22 stitches represents one side of your bag.

② Knit the 22 stitches on one needle, place a marker, knit the 22 stitches on the other needle, and place an end-of-round marker.

③ On the next round, begin increasing to shape the bottom of the bag as follows: *Knit 1, make 1, knit to 1 stitch before the marker, make 1, knit 1, slip marker. Repeat from * once.

④ Knit 1 round.

⑤ Repeat steps 3–4 until there are 88 total stitches (44 on each side). This will take 22 total rounds to complete.

MIDDLE OF BAG

FOR SINGLE-COLORED BAG A

① Knit 30 rounds, then go to the "Top of Bag" section on the next page.

FOR STRIPED BAG B

① Knit 10 rounds with color A. Cut yarn.

② Switch to color B and purl 1 round. Then knit 16 rounds.

③ Switch back to color A and knit 3 more rounds. Then go to the "Top of Bag" section below.

Tote Bag A

Tote Bag B

TOP OF BAG

1 Begin decreasing for the top of the bag as follows: *Knit 1, k2tog, knit to 3 stitches before marker, k2tog, knit 1, slip marker. Repeat from * once.

2 Knit 1 round.

3 Repeat steps 1–2 until 64 stitches remain (32 on each side). This will take 12 total rounds.

4 Knit 20 rounds.

5 Continuing in color A for Bag A and switching to color B for Bag B, create a garter stitch band as follows: *Purl 1 round, knit 1 round. Repeat from * once, then purl 1 more round.

6 Bind off loosely. Weave in all yarn ends.

Garter stitch band

FINISHING

1 To felt the bag, place it in the washing machine with a few pairs of jeans, old sneakers, or towels and a few tennis balls if you have them. Wool felts in the presence of heat and agitation, so an upright machine that causes a lot of agitation gives you better results. The jeans, sneakers, and tennis balls help create agitation as well. Add your preferred detergent and set the machine for a hot wash cycle.

2 After the wash cycle has ended, promptly remove the bag and check to see that it's fully felted. If you can see no light through the fabric and can no longer see the stitches, it is done. You may need to repeat these steps until the bag is fully felted.

NOTE: If you have a front-loading washer, it may take multiple cycles to get the amount of felting you desire. You can also take your project to a laundromat and felt it there. Doing so saves wear and tear on your machine, particularly if you have a front loader.

3 While the bag is still damp, use a sharp pair of scissors to create handles as follows: Cut a 5-inch-wide horizontal slit on one side of the bag about 1¼ inches from the top (see illustration). Repeat on the other side of the bag. Pull these handles firmly up and away from the bag to give them the desired shape.

4 Lay the bag flat on a towel in a warm, sunny location. Allow it to dry completely, flipping it over occasionally. This may take a couple of days, as the wool fibers are now thick and matted.

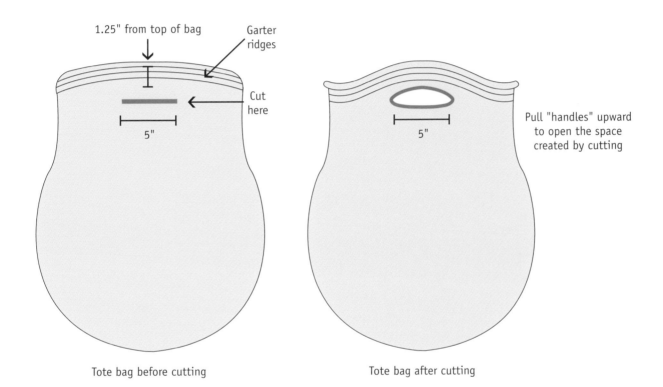

1.25" from top of bag

Garter ridges

Cut here

5"

Tote bag before cutting

5"

Pull "handles" upward to open the space created by cutting

Tote bag after cutting

Mittens for the Family

I live in New England, where a good pair of mittens is of great value in winter. Because they are so small and knit up quickly, mittens make an excellent project for new knitters to experiment on. Knit some for yourself and make some for others—mittens make excellent gifts.

Mittens A

Mittens B

Mittens C

Mittens D

Specifications

SIZE

XXS (XS, S, M, L, XL, XXL)

Circumference: 5½ (6, 6½, 7, 7½, 8, 8½) inches

YARN

You can use any weight of yarn, from heavy fingering through worsted, for this project. See the "Choose Your Yarn" section on page 150 for recommendations. The number of yards you need will vary depending on your gauge as well as the size and length of your mittens. The table below will give you a rough estimate of the yardage you may need.

Estimated Yardage Required for Mittens	
Gauge in Stockinette	**Approximate Yardage**
4 sts/inch	50–165 yards
5 sts/inch	70–205 yards
6 sts/inch	85–275 yards
7 sts/inch	90–300 yards
8 sts/inch	100–325 yards

Mitten A: Valley Yarns *Northampton Bulky* (100% wool, 109 yd. per skein), 2 skeins in color Dark Green Heather. These mittens were worked in plain stockinette in size XL at 4 stitches per inch.

Mitten B: Valley Yarns *Berkshire* (85% wool/15% alpaca, 141 yd. per skein), 1 skein in color Stone

Blue. These mittens were worked in plain stockinette in size L at 4 stitches per inch.

Mitten C: Foxfire Fiber *Upland Wool & Alpaca* (80% wool/20% prime alpaca, 135 yd. per skein), 1 skein in color Aster. These mittens were worked in a cable pattern in size S at 5 stitches per inch.

Mitten D: Valley Yarns *Valley Superwash DK* (100% extrafine superwash merino, 137 yd. per ball), 1 ball each in colors (A) Biscuit, (B) Teal, (C) Spring Leaf, and (D) Misty Lilac. These mittens were worked in striped stockinette in size XXS at 7 stitches per inch.

NEEDLES

Your choice of one of the following types of needles in the size needed to obtain your desired gauge:

One set of 4 or 5 double-pointed needles

Two 16-inch circular needles

One 32- to 40-inch circular needle

NOTE: See the "Choose a Circular Knitting Method" section on the next page for details on choosing needles for this project.

NOTIONS

Stitch markers
Cable needle, if working cable pattern shown on Mitten C
Stitch holder or short length of scrap yarn
Seaming needle

CABLE CHART FOR MITTEN C

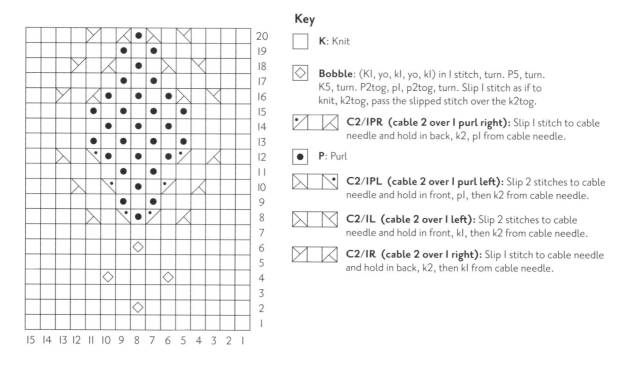

Key

☐	**K**: Knit
◇	**Bobble**: (K1, yo, k1, yo, k1) in 1 stitch, turn. P5, turn. K5, turn. P2tog, p1, p2tog, turn. Slip 1 stitch as if to knit, k2tog, pass the slipped stitch over the k2tog.
	C2/1PR (cable 2 over 1 purl right): Slip 1 stitch to cable needle and hold in back, k2, p1 from cable needle.
●	**P**: Purl
	C2/1PL (cable 2 over 1 purl left): Slip 2 stitches to cable needle and hold in front, p1, then k2 from cable needle.
	C2/1L (cable 2 over 1 left): Slip 2 stitches to cable needle and hold in front, k1, then k2 from cable needle.
	C2/1R (cable 2 over 1 right): Slip 1 stitch to cable needle and hold in back, k2, then k1 from cable needle.

Mitten C was created by working this cable chart centered on the back of the hand of each mitten.

Plan Your Mittens

CONSTRUCTION OVERVIEW

These mittens begin with a ribbed cuff that you work in the round. Then you work a few rounds of stockinette to create a smooth transition from the cuff to the hand. Next, you create a triangular insert called a *gusset* over a series of rounds to make room for the thumb joint on one side of the palm. Once this gusset is wide enough and long enough to cover the thumb joint, you place the gusset stitches on a stitch holder or piece of scrap yarn. You work the remaining stitches in the round to create the hand of the mitten. Then you shape the top of the mitten using decreases on each side. Finally, you return the gusset stitches to the knitting needles and work these stitches in the round to create the thumb of the mitten. You also decrease these stitches and finish them off.

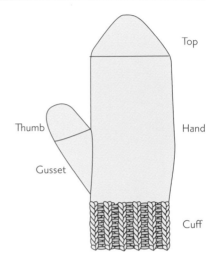

NOTE: Use the illustration on this page to familiarize yourself with mitten anatomy before you proceed to the mitten pattern.

CHOOSE A CIRCULAR KNITTING METHOD

You can work mittens with double-pointed needles, two short circular needles, or the magic-loop technique. A mitten has a small circumference, so you can't knit it on one short (16-inch) circular needle. It is easier to try on the mitten to check the fit when you work it using two circulars or the magic-loop method. Both of these methods also make it easier to transport your project. See Chapter 2 for details on the various circular knitting techniques.

CHOOSE A SIZE

Determine the hand circumference of the intended wearer by measuring around the palm just below the base of the fingers. Do not include the thumb in this measurement. If you like a snug-fitting mitten, use this measurement. If you prefer a looser mitten, add ¼ to ½ inch to the hand circumference for a bit of positive ease (see page 104 for more information about ease).

From the sizes listed on the previous page, select the mitten size that most closely corresponds to your calculated circumference. Your calculated value probably won't exactly match one of these sizes. If you want looser mittens, round your measurement up to the next size; if you want your mittens to be more snug, round your value down to the next size.

CHOOSE YOUR YARN

I recommend that you knit your mittens using a yarn made of a fiber that retains warmth when wet, such as wool, alpaca, mohair, or a blend of these yarns. In general it is best to avoid 100-percent cotton or acrylic fibers for mittens unless the wearer has an allergy to animal fibers. You can use blends containing some of those fibers, but keep in mind that the less animal fiber present, the less warmth will be retained and the more moisture will penetrate the mitten. Also, you may want to select a yarn with multiple plies to lessen the amount of pilling and increase wear. Consider using a superwash yarn if you are making mittens for children.

This pattern includes instructions for yarns that range from heavy fingering weight to worsted weight. Working with thicker yarns requires you to cast on fewer stitches and allows you to finish the work more quickly, but working with finer yarns enables you to create a more elegant mitten and use more detailed stitch patterns (see below).

CHOOSE YOUR STITCH PATTERN

Mittens are a great place to try out different techniques. Lacy stitch patterns are not a good choice for mittens (for obvious reasons—open holes do not make for warm fingers!). Knit-and-purl combinations and color-work designs work well as allover stitch patterns for the hand of the mitten. Stranded colorwork has the benefit of adding warmth. If you choose a knit-and-purl pattern, you may want to work the entire thumb (including the thumb gusset) in plain stockinette. Similarly, if you choose a colorwork stitch pattern, you may find it easier to work the entire thumb in a simple pattern, like alternating main and contrasting color stitches, and work only the hand stitches in the main stitch pattern.

If you choose a cable pattern, you can either use it as an allover pattern or just work the cables along the back of the hand. To do so, just work the chosen cable chart so that it is centered on the second half of the stitches, starting in the hand section (as was done with Mitten C). See Chapter 10 for possible stitch patterns to use on your mittens. Be sure to select a stitch pattern with a number of stitches that will fit evenly into your number of cast-on stitches.

DETERMINE YOUR GAUGE

Knit a swatch in your pattern stitch using your chosen yarn and the needle size recommended on the ball band (see the "Swatching for a Master Pattern" section on page 118). Consider swatching with a needle that is one or two sizes smaller than the ball-band recommendation to get a slightly tighter gauge. This will give you a denser fabric that will better withstand the elements. Continue swatching with different needle sizes until you find a density of fabric that you like.

Next, measure your gauge (see page 120) in stitches per inch. This pattern includes instructions for gauges from 4 to 8 stitches per inch. If your gauge is not a whole number, round your gauge value up for a slightly looser mitten or down for a slightly tighter mitten.

Make the Mittens

NOTE: The instructions below vary slightly for the right and left mitten. Be sure to follow the instructions for the mitten you are creating.

CUFF

① Using the long-tail cast-on (see page 28), cast on the number of stitches specified in the table below for your gauge and desired mitten size.

NOTE: If making striped Mitten D, cast on using color A.

Number of Stitches to Cast On							
Gauge	XXS	XS	S	M	L	XL	XXL
4 sts/inch	22	24	26	28	30	32	34
5 sts/inch	28	30	32	34	38	40	42
6 sts/inch	32	36	38	42	44	48	50
7 sts/inch	38	42	46	48	52	56	60
8 sts/inch	44	48	52	56	60	64	68

② Arrange your stitches on the needles according to your chosen circular knitting method (see Chapter 2). Join for working in the round, being careful not to twist the cast on around the needles. Place a marker to indicate the end of the round.

③ *Knit 1, purl 1; repeat from * to the end of the round.

④ Continue working in knit 1, purl 1 rib until the cuff of the mitten measures 2 (2¼, 2½, 2½, 2¾, 2¾, 3) inches.

HAND

NOTE: In this pattern, I worked every make 1 increase as a backward-loop make 1 (see page 233). You can use another increase if you prefer.

① Change to stockinette stitch (or your chosen stitch pattern) and work for ¼ (¼, ½, ½, ½, ½, ½) inch. The first half of your stitches will become the palm of the mitten; the second half will be the back of the mitten.

For cabled Mitten C, work the cable pattern (see page 148) centered on the back of the hand.

For striped Mitten D, work the entire hand and thumb of the mitten in the following stripe pattern:

    3 rounds of color B
    3 rounds of color C
    3 rounds of color D
    3 rounds of color A

NOTE: For tips on working stripes in the round, see page 85.

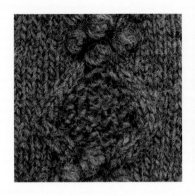

Cabled stitch pattern—Mitten C

Stripe pattern—Mitten D

② On the next round, begin increasing for the thumb gusset as follows:

Right mitten: Knit 1, place beginning-of-gusset marker, make 1, knit 2, make 1, place end-of-gusset marker, knit to the end of the round.

Left mitten: Knit to 3 stitches before the halfway point of the round, place beginning-of-gusset marker, make 1, knit 2, make 1, place end-of-gusset marker, knit to the end of the round.

Thumb gusset—Mitten A

③ Knit 1 round.

④ Knit to the first marker, slip marker, make 1, knit to the next marker, make 1, slip marker, knit to the end of the round.

⑤ Repeat steps 3–4 until the specified number of gusset stitches from the table at right is present between the two gusset markers.

Number of Gusset Stitches between Markers							
Gauge	**XXS**	**XS**	**S**	**M**	**L**	**XL**	**XXL**
4 sts/inch	10	10	10	12	12	12	14
5 sts/inch	10	12	12	12	14	16	16
6 sts/inch	12	14	14	16	16	18	18
7 sts/inch	14	16	16	18	20	20	22
8 sts/inch	16	18	20	20	22	24	26

6 Put the mitten on your (or the intended wearer's) hand with the cuff positioned on your wrist so that the gusset stitches are over your thumb joint. Check whether the top of your work reaches your "thumb web" (the point where your thumb joins your upper palm). If not, work more rounds in stockinette without increasing until you reach this point.

7 Knit to the first gusset marker and remove it. Then place the gusset stitches (those between the markers) onto a stitch holder or piece of scrap yarn and remove the second gusset marker. Set these stitches aside to be worked later for the thumb. Using a backward-loop cast-on (see page 234), cast on 2 new stitches to cross the gap created by the removal of the gusset stitches, and knit to the end of the round. The total number of stitches on the needles should now equal the original number of cast-on stitches.

8 Work in stockinette stitch until the mitten reaches the specified distance (see the table below) from the tip of the middle finger when you try it on.

When working the last round, place a marker at the halfway point of the round (after the first half of the stitches).

Distance from Tip of Middle Finger							
Gauge	**XXS**	**XS**	**S**	**M**	**L**	**XL**	**XXL**
4 sts/"	1"	1"	1¼"	1¼"	1½"	1½"	1½"
5 sts/"	1"	1¼"	1¼"	1½"	1½"	1½"	1¾"
6 sts/"	1"	1¼"	1¼"	1½"	1½"	1½"	1¾"
7 sts/"	1¼"	1¼"	1¼"	1½"	1½"	1½"	1¾"
8 sts/"	1¼"	1¼"	1¼"	1½"	1½"	1½"	1¾"

TOP OF MITTEN

① K2tog, knit to 2 stitches before marker, ssk, slip marker, k2tog, knit to 2 stitches before end of round, ssk.

Decreases at top—Mitten A

② Repeat the previous round until the correct number of stitches (see the table at right) remain at the top of the mitten.

③ Cut the yarn, leaving an 8-inch tail, and thread onto a seaming needle. Run the yarn through all of the remaining stitches and pull snugly to tighten. Take the yarn end to the inside and weave it in.

Number of Stitches Remaining at Top of Mitten							
Gauge	**XXS**	**XS**	**S**	**M**	**L**	**XL**	**XXL**
4 sts/inch	6	8	6	8	6	8	6
5 sts/inch	8	6	8	6	6	8	6
6 sts/inch	8	8	6	6	8	8	6
7 sts/inch	6	6	6	8	8	8	8
8 sts/inch	8	8	8	8	8	8	8

THUMB

① Slip the gusset stitches from the stitch holder (or scrap yarn) back onto your needle(s).

② Knit across the thumb stitches, then pick up and knit 2 stitches across the gap. Knit 1 more stitch, then place a marker to indicate the end of the round.

③ Knit to 4 stitches before the end of the round, ssk, k2tog.

④ Work in stockinette on all stitches until the tip of the mitten's thumb measures about $1/4$ inch below the tip of your thumb when you try it on.

Thumb—Mitten A

5 Remove the end-of-round marker and work the thumb decreases as follows: *Knit 1, k2tog; repeat from * until 8 total stitches remain on the thumb. Then *k2tog; repeat from * until 4 stitches remain.

6 Cut the yarn, leaving an 8-inch tail. Thread this tail onto a seaming needle and pull it through all remaining stitches of the thumb. Pull snugly, then take the yarn to the inside and weave it in.

FINISHING

1 Weave in any remaining loose ends.

2 Make a second mitten per the directions above, making sure to follow the instructions for the opposite hand.

3 Wash and block mittens, if desired.

Basic Socks, Kids to Adults

Socks are a lot of fun to knit and useful as well. I often hear people say that they don't think they can knit socks because socks are "too hard." They really aren't. This isn't to say that they're easy, but if you can increase, decrease, and knit in the round, you can knit a sock!

Socks A

Socks B

Specifications

SIZE

XXS (XS, S, M, L, XL, XXL)

Circumference: 5½ (6½, 7½, 8, 8½, 9, 10) inches

YARN

You can use any weight of yarn for this project. See the "Choose Your Yarn" section on the next page for recommendations. The number of yards you need will vary depending on your gauge as well as the size and length of your socks. The table at right will give you a rough estimate of the yardage you may need.

Sock A: Lorna's Laces *Shepherd Sock* (80% superwash wool/20% nylon, 435 yd. per skein), 1 skein in color Woodlawn. This sock was worked in size XXS at 8 stitches per inch.

Sock B: Lion Brand *Superwash Merino Cashmere* (72% superwash merino/15% nylon/13% cashmere, 87 yd. per skein), 3 skeins in color Slate. This sock was worked in size M at 5 stitches per inch.

Estimated Yardages for Socks	
Gauge in Stockinette	**Approximate Yardage**
5 sts/inch	95–350 yards
6 sts/inch	140–500 yards
7 sts/inch	150–550 yards
8 sts/inch	160–600 yards
9 sts/inch	180–650 yards

NEEDLES

Your choice of one of the following types of needles in the size needed to obtain your desired gauge:

> One set of 4 or 5 double-pointed needles
> Two 16-inch circular needles
> One 32- to 40-inch circular needle

NOTE: See the "Choose a Circular Knitting Method" section on the next page for details on choosing needles for this project.

NOTIONS

Stitch markers
Seaming needle

Plan Your Socks

CONSTRUCTION OVERVIEW

You work the socks in this pattern from the cuff down to the toe. You typically work the cuff of a sock in a rib pattern so that it hugs the leg. Next, you work the leg in the desired stitch pattern; in this pattern I continue the simple rib used on the cuff throughout the sock. The heel flap, a rectangular section worked back and forth in rows to cover the back of the heel, is worked next. You then turn the heel to create a cup shape that will fit over the bottom of the heel. You return to working in the round by picking up gusset stitches along the sides of the heel flap. A gusset is a triangular insert in your fabric that makes room for the heel. You gradually decrease away the gusset stitches until your sock is back to the original number of cast-on stitches. You then work the foot to the desired length, work decreases at either side of the foot to shape the toes, and close the end of the sock with Kitchener stitch.

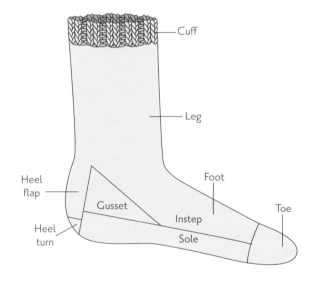

CHOOSE A CIRCULAR KNITTING METHOD

You can work socks with double-pointed needles, two short circular needles, or the magic-loop technique. A sock has a small circumference, so you can't knit it on one short (16-inch) circular needle. It is easier to try on the sock to check the fit when you work it using two circulars or the magic-loop method. Also, both of these methods make it easier to transport your project. See Chapter 2 for details on the various circular knitting techniques.

CHOOSE A SIZE

Determine the foot circumference of the intended wearer by measuring around the ball of the foot at the widest part. Since socks should fit snugly, you need to plan for a bit of negative ease. Subtract roughly 10 percent, or about ½–1 inch, from the foot circumference (see page 104 for more information about ease). If you're using a very stretchy stitch pattern (like a rib), subtract more; if you're using a less elastic stitch pattern (like a wide cable), subtract less.

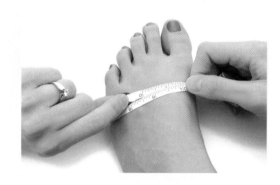

From the list of sizes on page 157, (see "Size"), select the sock size that mostly closely corresponds with your calculated circumference from above. Your calculated value probably won't exactly match one of these sizes. If you want looser socks, round your value to the next size up; if you want tighter socks, round your value to the next size down.

CHOOSE YOUR YARN

I recommend that you knit your socks using a yarn made of a fiber that has both elasticity and durability. Wool can provide elasticity and is my favorite fiber for sock knitting. Durability in most commercial sock yarns comes from nylon. There are some natural alternatives to wool, with silk and mohair being the most noteworthy. Both increase the longevity of the yarn when worn against the skin and subjected to the abrasion that socks experience. Most commercial sock yarns are made of superwash wool, which makes them easier to launder.

This pattern includes instructions for yarns that range from fingering weight to worsted weight. Working with thicker yarns requires you to cast on fewer stitches and allows you to finish the work more quickly. It also creates a thicker, cozier sock that is good for cold winter nights, but not one that fits comfortably under regular shoes. Working with finer sock yarns enables you to create 3-season socks that will fit in your shoes comfortably.

CHOOSE YOUR STITCH PATTERN

Although the samples presented here are worked in rib throughout, socks are a great project to try out different stitch patterns. Stripes, cables, lace, knit-and-purl combinations, and stranded colorwork all work well on socks. See Chapter 10 for possible stitch patterns to use on your socks. Be sure your number of cast-on stitches is evenly divisible by the number of stitches in any selected stitch pattern.

Cables work well with any weight of yarn, although they can get bulky with heavier yarn. Also, be aware that cables are less stretchy than plain ribbing, so don't include too much negative ease when determining which size to make. You can use cables as an allover pattern or intersperse them with columns of ribbing or reverse stockinette stitch. In either case, work the sole of the sock in plain stockinette.

Colorwork patterns are a good choice if you want to add thickness and warmth. They also decrease the elasticity of your socks, so don't include negative ease when determining which size to make. It is easiest to work the heel in a solid color and then return to the colorwork pattern for the gusset. However, be aware that the number of stitches per round will continually decrease throughout the gusset section. You may want to consider how to incorporate the decreases into your pattern.

Lacy stitch patterns are a good choice for lightweight yarns. They give a touch of femininity to your finished socks. Unlike cable and colorwork patterns, lace patterns tend to be fairly stretchy, so include a good amount of negative ease. The heel, sole, and toe of the sock will be more durable if you work them in plain stockinette stitch. Other good choices for socks are knit-and-purl combinations and stripes (see page 85 for tips on working stripes in the round).

DETERMINE YOUR GAUGE

Knit a swatch in your pattern stitch using your chosen yarn and the needle size recommended on the ball band (see the "Swatching for a Master Pattern" section on page 118). Consider swatching with a needle one or two sizes smaller than the ball-band recommendation to get a slightly tighter gauge. Doing so will give you a denser fabric that will wear better on the soles of your socks. Continue swatching with different needle sizes until you find a density of fabric that you like.

Next, measure your gauge (see page 120) in stitches per inch. This pattern includes instructions for gauges from 5 to 9 stitches per inch. If your gauge is not a whole number, round your gauge value up for a slightly looser sock or down for a slightly tighter sock.

Make the Socks

LEG

1 Using the long-tail cast-on (see page 28), cast on the number of stitches specified in the table below for your gauge and desired size.

Number of Stitches to Cast On							
Gauge	XXS	XS	S	M	L	XL	XXL
5 sts/inch	28	32	36	40	44	48	52
6 sts/inch	32	40	44	48	52	56	60
7 sts/inch	40	44	52	56	60	64	72
8 sts/inch	44	52	60	64	68	72	80
9 sts/inch	48	60	68	72	76	80	92

Leg—Sock A

2 Arrange your stitches on the needles according to your chosen circular knitting method (see Chapter 2). Join to work in the round, being careful not to twist your cast on around the needles. Place a stitch marker to indicate the end of the round.

3 *Knit 1, purl 1. Repeat from * to the beginning of the round.

4 Continue working in knit 1, purl 1 rib until the leg measures 4½ (5, 5½, 6, 6, 6½, 6½) inches from the cast-on edge.

DIVIDE FOR THE HEEL

1 Starting at the beginning of the round, slip the number of stitches specified in the table at right onto one needle. You will work these stitches for the heel as described in the "Heel Flap" section on the next page.

2 Hold aside the remaining stitches to be worked later as the instep (top of the foot).

NOTE: If you are using double-pointed needles, arrange these stitches on two needles or transfer them to a piece of waste yarn, if you prefer.

Number of Stitches in Heel Flap							
Gauge	XXS	XS	S	M	L	XL	XXL
5 sts/inch	14	16	18	20	22	24	26
6 sts/inch	16	20	22	24	26	28	30
7 sts/inch	20	22	26	28	30	32	36
8 sts/inch	22	26	30	32	34	36	40
9 sts/inch	24	30	34	36	38	40	46

HEEL FLAP

You work the heel flap back and forth in rows as follows:

1 (RS): *Slip 1 as if to purl, knit 1. Repeat from * to the end of the heel needle. Turn your work.

2 (WS): Slip 1 as if to purl, purl to the end of the heel needle. Turn.

3 Repeat steps 1–2 until the heel flap measures 2 (2¼, 2¼, 2¼, 2½, 2½, 2¾) inches. End having just completed a wrong-side row.

Heel flap (back view)—Sock A

HEEL TURN

Continue working back and forth in rows on the heel stitches as follows:

1 (RS): Slip 1, knit across the number of stitches specified in the table below, ssk, knit 1. Turn.

Number of Stitches to Knit Before Decreasing							
Gauge	XXS	XS	S	M	L	XL	XXL
5 sts/inch	8	9	10	11	12	13	14
6 sts/inch	9	11	12	13	14	15	16
7 sts/inch	11	12	14	15	16	17	19
8 sts/inch	12	14	16	17	18	19	21
9 sts/inch	13	16	18	19	20	21	24

Heel turn at base of heel flap—Sock A

2 (WS): Slip 1 as if to purl, purl 5, p2tog, purl 1. Turn.

NOTE: Slipping the first stitch of every row creates a series of elongated stitches along both edges of the heel flap. This makes it easier to pick up stitches for the gusset below.

3 (RS): Slip 1 as if to purl, knit 6, ssk, knit 1. Turn.

4 (WS): Slip 1 as if to purl, purl 7, p2tog, purl 1. Turn.

5 (RS): Slip 1 as if to purl, knit 8, ssk, knit 1. Turn.

6 Continue in rows as established, always working one more stitch than the row before and each time working a decrease to close the gap that appears on either side of the center stitches of the heel flap, until you have used all picked-up stitches. End having completed a wrong-side row.

NOTE: For some sock sizes, you won't have enough stitches to end the last two rows with a knit 1 or purl 1. These rows will end with an ssk or k2tog.

You should have the number of stitches specified in the table at right remaining on the heel needle.

Number of Heel Stitches Remaining After Turning Heel							
Gauge	XXS	XS	S	M	L	XL	XXL
5 sts/inch	10	10	12	12	14	14	16
6 sts/inch	10	12	14	14	16	16	18
7 sts/inch	12	14	16	16	18	18	20
8 sts/inch	14	16	18	18	20	20	22
9 sts/inch	14	18	20	20	22	22	26

PICK UP STITCHES FOR GUSSET

Pick up stitches along the sides of the heel flap and resume working in the round as follows:

1 Knit across the heel stitches. Using the same needle, pick up and knit 1 stitch in each slipped stitch along the edge of the heel flap. Pick up and knit an extra stitch in the corner where the heel flap meets the instep. Note the number of stitches you picked up.

2 Place a marker to show the beginning of the instep. With another needle, work across the instep stitches in the established knit 1, purl 1 rib. Place another marker to show the end of the instep.

Gusset stitches at side of heel flap—Sock A

TIP

If you're using a set of four double-pointed needles, it is best to arrange the instep stitches on one needle, with the remaining stitches split evenly between two other needles. With a set of five dpns, you can split the instep stitches between two needles. If you're using the magic-loop or two-circulars method, divide your stitches so that the instep stitches are on one half of the cable (or one needle) and the gusset and heel stitches are on the other.

Basic Socks, Kids to Adults *(continued)*

3 Pick up and knit 1 stitch in the corner where the instep meets the heel flap. Then pick up and knit 1 stitch in each slipped stitch along the other side of the heel flap. Make sure the total number of picked-up stitches on each side of the heel flap is the same.

4 Knit the number of stitches specified in the table at right across the heel stitches. Place a marker to indicate that the center of the heel is now the end of the round.

Number of Stitches to Knit Across Heel to End of Round							
Gauge	XXS	XS	S	M	L	XL	XXL
5 sts/inch	5	5	6	6	7	7	8
6 sts/inch	5	6	7	7	8	8	9
7 sts/inch	6	7	8	8	9	9	10
8 sts/inch	7	8	9	9	10	10	11
9 sts/inch	7	9	10	10	11	11	13

GUSSET DECREASES

1 Knit to 3 stitches before the first marker, k2tog, knit 1, slip marker. Work instep stitches in the established rib pattern to the next marker. Slip marker, knit 1, ssk, knit to the end of the round (center of heel).

2 Knit to the first marker, slip marker, work the instep stitches in pattern as established to the next marker, slip marker, knit to the end of the round.

3 Repeat steps 1–2 until the number of stitches shown in the table below remains.

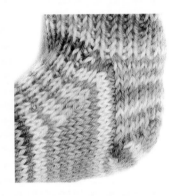

Line of decreases at gusset—Sock A

FOOT

1 Knit to the first marker, slip marker, work the instep stitches in pattern as established to the next marker, slip marker, knit to the end of the round.

2 Repeat Step 1, keeping the sole stitches (bottom of the foot) in stockinette and the instep stitches in pattern, until the foot of the sock measures 1 (1¼, 1½, 1½, 1¾, 2, 2¼) inches less than the total foot length of the intended wearer.

Total Number of Stitches Remaining After Gusset Decreases							
Gauge	XXS	XS	S	M	L	XL	XXL
5 sts/inch	28	32	36	40	44	48	52
6 sts/inch	32	40	44	48	52	56	60
7 sts/inch	40	44	52	56	60	64	72
8 sts/inch	44	52	60	64	68	72	80
9 sts/inch	48	60	68	72	76	80	92

TOE

Work all stitches in stockinette while decreasing for the toe as follows:

1. *Knit to 3 stitches before the marker, k2tog, knit 1, slip marker, knit 1, ssk. Repeat from * once. Knit to the end of the round.

2. Knit 1 round with no decreases.

3. Work steps 1–2 the total number of times specified in the table below.

Toe decreases—Sock A

	Number of Decreases on Alternate Rounds for the Toe	
Gauge	Number of Times to Work Decreases on Alternate Rounds	Total Number of Stitches Remaining
5 sts/inch	2 (3, 4, 4, 4, 5, 5)	20 (20, 20, 24, 28, 28, 32)
6 sts/inch	3 (3, 4, 4, 5, 6, 6)	20 (28, 28, 32, 32, 32, 36)
7 sts/inch	4 (5, 5, 5, 6, 7, 8)	24 (24, 32, 36, 36, 36, 40)
8 sts/inch	4 (5, 6, 6, 7, 8, 9)	28 (32, 36, 40, 40, 40, 44)
9 sts/inch	5 (6, 7, 7, 8, 9, 10)	28 (36, 40, 44, 44, 44, 52)

4. Work just Step 1 (decreasing every round) until 12 (12, 16, 16, 20) stitches remain. Then knit to the first marker (end of the sole).

5. If you're using double-pointed needles, rearrange the stitches so that the remaining sole stitches are on one needle and the remaining instep stitches are on another needle. (For the other methods, your stitches should already be arranged in this way.)

6. Graft the toe together using Kitchener stitch (see page 237). Weave in all yarn ends.

   Repeat the instructions above to make a second sock.

Grafted area (Kitchener stitch)—
Sock A

CHAPTER 8

Advanced Projects

Who doesn't love a hand-knit sweater? Here you will find sweaters to knit for every member of the family, from babies to adults. Knitting sweaters on circular needles means little or no seaming, so these sweaters save you time in finishing.

Infant's Cardigan, Hat, and Booties

Babies are fun to knit for. This adorable set in three sizes will fit babies from birth to age 12 months. Knit the set in a luxury yarn for a special occasion or in a simple, durable yarn for everyday wear. You knit the body of this sweater back and forth from the bottom up, and work the sleeves from the top down—there is no seaming of the sleeve to the body when you're finished. And if the sweater fits but the sleeves are too long or short, you can easily make adjustments.

Sweater Set A

Sweater Set B

Specifications

SIZE
Cardigan chest circumference: 19½ (21, 22½) inches
Hat circumference: 14½ (16, 17½) inches
Bootie circumference: 5¾ inches

YARN
500 (550,620) yards of DK-weight yarn, 295 (320, 380) yards for the cardigan, 85 (110, 120) yards for the hat, and 120 yards for the booties

Sweater Set A: Lorna's Laces *Honor* (70% baby alpaca/30% silk, 275 yd. per skein), 2 (2, 3) skeins in color Calumet

Sweater Set B: Valley Yarns *Valley Superwash DK* (100% extra-fine merino superwash, 137 yd. per ball), 4 (4, 5) balls in color Misty Lilac

NEEDLES
US 5 24- to 32-inch circular needle, or size needed to obtain gauge

US 6 24- to 32-inch circular needle, or one size larger than that needed to obtain gauge
Set of 4 or 5 US 5 double-pointed needles
Set of 4 or 5 US 6 double-pointed needles
(The length and type of needles required will vary depending on the circular knitting method you use. See the "Plan the Infant Sweater Set" section on the next page for details.)

NOTIONS
Locking stitch markers
Stitch holders or waste yarn
Seaming needle
3–7 buttons for cardigan
Sewing thread to match yarn

GAUGE
5½ stitches × 6½ rows per inch, worked in stockinette stitch on the smaller needles

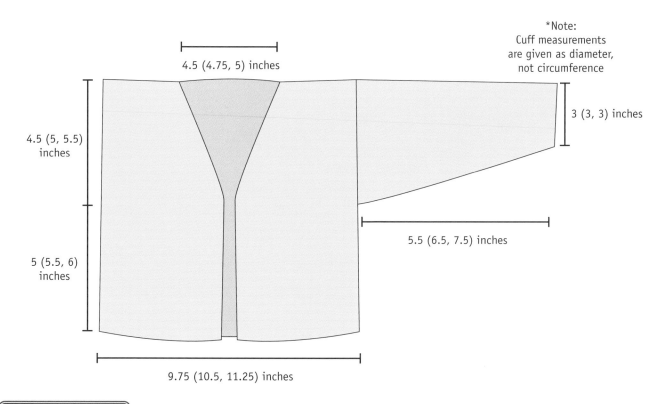

4.5 (4.75, 5) inches

*Note:
Cuff measurements
are given as diameter,
not circumference

3 (3, 3) inches

4.5 (5, 5.5)
inches

5 (5.5, 6)
inches

5.5 (6.5, 7.5) inches

9.75 (10.5, 11.25) inches

Stitch Pattern

BLACKBERRY PATTERN STITCH

When you are working in the round, read the chart from right to left for all rounds. When you are working flat, read the chart from right to left for right-side rows and from left to right for wrong-side rows. See page 83 for information about reading charts when working in the round versus flat.

Key

$\boxed{V}$	(P1, k1, p1) in 1 stitch
$\boxed{/\!\!\backslash}$	K3tog
(gray)	No stitch
•	**RS:** Purl **WS:** Knit

Plan the Infant Sweater Set

CONSTRUCTION OVERVIEW

At first glance, this sweet little sweater appears to defy the very intent of this book; you work the body back and forth in flat knitting. A closer look reveals this garment to be a blend of flat and circular techniques. Once you complete the body and seam the shoulders, you pick up stitches around the armholes for the sleeves, which you work in the round from the top down. When the sweater is done, there are no seams to sew, which means less time in finishing. You work the hat and matching booties in the round. Note that there is no shaping in the booties; you knit them as simple tubes.

CIRCULAR KNITTING METHOD

You can work the body and button band of the cardigan flat using a 24- to 32-inch circular needle, while you can work the sleeves, hat, and booties in the round with double-pointed needles. Alternatively, if you use the magic-loop method, you can knit the entire set with a 32- to 40-inch circular needle. This is the method I prefer. Whichever method you choose, note that you will need two sizes of needles: a smaller needle for stockinette and a larger needle for the stitch pattern.

YARN SELECTION

Choosing yarn for baby things can be a difficult task. On the one hand, knitters love to pair soft and luscious yarns with fresh newborn skin. On the other hand, new moms may prefer a garment that they can easily wash and dry. The two yarns here represent the best of both worlds. One is superwash wool, which makes its way into the washing machine with ease. The other is a soft and luxurious blend of alpaca and silk that requires hand-washing, but so perfectly matches the softness of babies that it begs to be used here.

Make the Cardigan

BODY

1. With the smaller circular needle, cast on 104 (112, 120) stitches using the long-tail cast-on (see page 28). Do not join; you will work the body back and forth in rows.

2. Knit 5 rows, ending with a wrong-side row.

3. Change to the larger circular needle and work in the blackberry pattern stitch (see previous page for stitch pattern) until the piece measures 4½ (5, 5½) inches from the cast-on edge. End having completed a wrong-side row.

4. Change to the smaller circular needle and knit 4 rows.

Blackberry pattern stitch

Upper Back

1. Divide the body stitches as follows: Knit 26 (28, 30) stitches, then slip the stitches just worked to a stitch holder or piece of waste yarn to be worked later as the right front of the cardigan. Knit the next 52 (56, 60) stitches for the back, then slip the remaining 26 (28, 30) stitches to a stitch holder or piece of waste yarn and hold them aside to be worked later as the left front of the cardigan.

2. Working only on the 52 (56, 60) back stitches, work in stockinette stitch until the back measures $9\frac{1}{2}$ ($10\frac{1}{2}$, $11\frac{1}{2}$) inches from the cast-on edge. Cut yarn, leaving a 10-inch tail. Leave these stitches on the needle.

Upper Fronts (R/L)

1. Transfer the right front stitches onto one of the small double-pointed needles.

2. With the right side facing, attach a new ball of yarn and knit across the 26 (28, 30) stitches of the right front.

3. Continue to work in stockinette stitch until the right front measures 6 ($6\frac{1}{2}$, 7) inches from the cast-on edge. End having completed a wrong-side row.

4. Begin shaping the V-neck as follows: K1, ssk, knit to the end of the row. Purl 1 row.

5. Repeat Step 4 11 (12, 13) more times—14 (15, 16) stitches remain.

6. Work even on these stitches until the right front measures $9\frac{1}{2}$ ($10\frac{1}{2}$, $11\frac{1}{2}$) inches from the cast-on edge. Then slip the stitches to a stitch holder or a piece of waste yarn.

7. Cut yarn, leaving a 10-inch tail. Then repeat steps 2–6 to shape the left front, but work the decrease rows as follows: Knit to the last 3 stitches, k2tog, k1. When the left front is complete, leave the stitches on the needle. Do not cut yarn.

Decreases along neck edge

Join the Shoulders

1 Turn the sweater inside out and arrange the work so that the front and back shoulder stitches are aligned.

2 Using the yarn still attached to the left front, work a three-needle bind-off (see page 236) to join the first 14 (15, 16) stitches of the back to the 14 (15, 16) stitches of the left front.

3 Bind off the next 24 (26, 28) stitches for the back of the neck.

4 Transfer the right front stitches to one of the small double-pointed needles and use the three-needle bind-off to join the remaining 14 (15, 16) back stitches to the right front.

5 Turn the work right side out. Cut yarn, leaving a 10-inch tail.

SLEEVES

1 Using the smaller double-pointed needles, pick up and knit 50 (55, 60) stitches around one of the armholes, beginning at the underarm. Join to work in the round, placing a marker at the center of the underarm to indicate the end of the round.

2 Knit 4 rounds.

3 Work sleeve decreases at the underarm as follows: K1, ssk, knit to 3 stitches before the marker, k2tog, k1—2 stitches decreased.

4 Knit 2 rounds.

5 Repeat steps 3–4, 8 (10, 12) more times—32 (33, 34) stitches remain.

6 Work in stockinette stitch until the sleeve measures 5 (6, 7) inches from pick-up edge, or ½ inch less than the desired finished length.

Front/back shoulder join

Where sleeve meets body

Decreases along length of sleeve

7 Purl 1 round, knit 1 round, purl 1 round.

8 Bind off loosely.

9 Repeat steps 1–8 to create the other sleeve.

BUTTON BAND

1 With the smaller circular needle and right side facing, beginning at lower right edge of body, pick up and knit 33 (36, 39) stitches along right front opening, 24 (26, 28) stitches along right V-neck, 24 (26, 28) stitches along back neck edge, 24 (26, 28) stitches along left V-neck, and 33 (36, 39) stitches along left front edge—138 (150, 162) total stitches.

2 Knit 3 rows.

3 Use locking stitch markers to indicate the location of each desired buttonhole. The number and placement of the buttonholes is up to you.

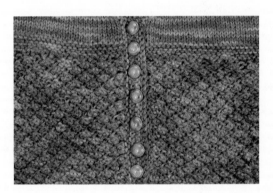

4 *Knit to a buttonhole marker, remove marker, k2tog, yarn over; repeat from * until you have worked all buttonholes. Then knit to the end of the row.

5 Knit 3 more rows.

6 Bind off all stitches.

FINISHING

1 Weave in all yarn ends.

2 Wash and block the cardigan before attaching buttons.

3 Use sewing thread to sew buttons into place on button band opposite buttonholes.

Make the Hat

1. With the smaller double-pointed needles, cast on 80 (88, 96) stitches using the long-tail cast-on (see page 28). Join to work in the round, being sure not to twist the cast-on edge around the needles. Place marker to indicate the end of the round.

2. *Purl 1 round, knit 1 round; repeat from * once, then purl 1 more round.

3. Change to the larger double-pointed needles and work in blackberry pattern stitch (see page 169) until the hat measures about 3¼ (3¾, 4¼) inches from the cast-on edge. End having completed round 2 or 4 of the stitch pattern.

4. Change to the smaller double-pointed needles and knit 1 round while placing markers for the crown decreases as follows. *Knit 10 (11, 12) stitches, place marker; repeat from * to the end of the round.

5. Knit 1 round.

6. *Knit to 2 stitches before marker, k2tog; repeat from * to end of round—8 stitches decreased.

7. Repeat steps 5–6 until 16 stitches remain.

8. *K2tog; repeat from * to the end of the round—8 stitches remain.

9. Cut yarn, leaving a 10-inch tail. Thread the tail onto a seaming needle and draw through the remaining stitches. Pull tightly to cinch. Take the yarn tails to the inside of the hat and weave in loose ends.

10. Wash and block if desired.

Hats A and B

Purl ridges and pattern stitch

Decreases

Make the Booties

These socks are presented in only one size.

CUFF

1. With the smaller double-pointed needles, cast on 32 stitches using the long-tail cast-on (see page 28). Join for working in the round, being sure not to twist the cast on. Place a marker to indicate the end of the round.

2. *Purl 1 round, knit 1 round. Repeat from * once, then purl 1 more round.

3. Change to the larger double-pointed needles and work in blackberry pattern stitch (see page 169) until the sock measures about 2 inches from the cast-on edge. End having completed round 2 or 4 of the stitch pattern.

4. Change to the smaller double-pointed needles and *knit 1 round, purl 1 round; repeat from * once.

LEG AND FOOT

1. Work in knit 1, purl 1 rib until the sock measures 5 inches from the cast-on edge.

2. K11, k2tog, k17, k2tog—30 stitches remain.

3. Knit 1 round while placing markers for toe decreases as follows. *K6, place marker; repeat from * to the end of the round.

4. *Knit to 2 stitches before marker, k2tog, slip marker; repeat from * to the end of the round—5 stitches decreased.

5. Knit 1 round.

6. Repeat steps 4–5 until 5 stitches remain, ending with the final decrease round.

7. Cut yarn, leaving a 10-inch tail. Thread the tail onto a seaming needle and draw through the remaining 5 stitches. Pull tightly to cinch. Take the yarn tails to the inside of the sock and weave in loose ends.

8. Repeat steps 1–7 to make a matching bootie.

9. Wash and block if desired.

Booties A and B

Patterned cuff of bootie

Toe of bootie

175

Kid's Striped Pullover

Single stripe, multiple stripes, or stripes of your own design—this simple children's drop-shoulder pullover can become anything you want it to be.

Striped Pullover A

Striped Pullover B

Specifications

SIZE
Chest circumference: 26 (28, 30) inches

YARN
600 (745, 895) yards of worsted-weight yarn

Pullover A: Blue Moon Fiber Arts *Socks That Rock Heavyweight* (100% superwash merino, 350 yd. per skein), 2 (2, 3) skeins of color (A) Beryl, 1 (1, 1) skein of color (B) Oregon Red Clover Honey

Pullover B: Berroco *Pure Merino* (100% extra-fine merino wool, 92 yd. per ball), 3 (3, 4) balls of color (A) Brick 1 (2, 2) balls each of (B) Kale, (D) Copper, 2 (3, 3) balls each of (C) Resin, (E) Cadet

NEEDLES
US 5 24-inch circular needle, or size needed to obtain gauge
Set of 4 or 5 US 5 double-pointed needles
(The length and type of needles required will vary depending on the circular knitting method you use. See the "Plan the Pullover" section on the next page for details.)

NOTIONS
Stitch markers
Seaming needle
Stitch holders or waste yarn

GAUGE
5 stitches × 7 rows per inch, worked in stockinette stitch in the round

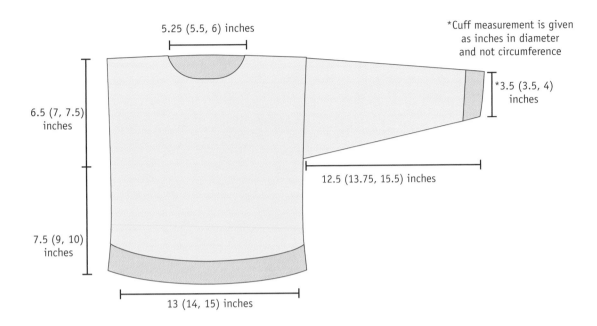

5.25 (5.5, 6) inches

*Cuff measurement is given
as inches in diameter
and not circumference

6.5 (7, 7.5)
inches

*3.5 (3.5, 4)
inches

12.5 (13.75, 15.5) inches

7.5 (9, 10)
inches

13 (14, 15) inches

Plan the Pullover

CONSTRUCTION OVERVIEW

You work the sweater in the round from the bottom to the underarm. You then divide the front and back and work flat to the shoulder, where you use a three-needle bind-off to join front and back. You then pick up sleeve stitches around the perimeter of the armhole, and work the sleeves in the round from the top down. You do this for two reasons: first, there is no need to seam or otherwise attach the sleeves to the body, and second, should the wearer grow more quickly in arm length than in circumference, you can release the sleeves from the bind-off and lengthen them.

CIRCULAR KNITTING METHOD

You can work the body of this sweater with one 24-inch circular needle in the traditional method and then use double-pointed needles to work the sleeves. My preferred method is to work both the body and the sleeves in the magic-loop method on one 40-inch circular needle.

YARN SELECTION

Any durable yarn would work for this child's sweater, but for this project I chose superwash wool yarns. Superwash yarns are able to withstand the rigors of children at play and can be tossed into the washer after contact with dirt, grass, or spilled ice cream. That is an important concern for many parents; hand-washing and modern lifestyles don't always go hand in hand!

Kid's Striped Pullover *(continued)*

Knit the Pullover

BODY

① Using the circular needle, cast on 128 (140, 148) stitches in color A using the long-tail cast-on (see page 28). Join for working in the round, being careful not to twist the cast on around the needle. Place a marker to indicate the end of the round.

② Work in knit 2, purl 2 rib until the work measures 1½ (2, 2) inches from cast-on edge.

③ Go to the directions for the desired stripe pattern below.

Bottom edge of Striped Pullover B

STRIPE FOR SWEATER A (SINGLE-STRIPE)

① Still in color A, change to stockinette stitch and work until the body measures 4¾ (6¼, 7¾) inches from cast-on edge. Cut yarn, leaving a 10-inch tail.

② Change to color B and work 16 rounds. Cut yarn, leaving a 10-inch tail.

③ Return to color A and work until the body measures 7½ (9, 10½) inches from cast-on edge, then go to the "Back" section on the next page.

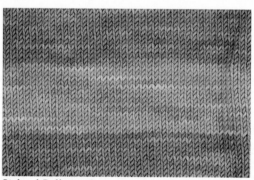

Striped Pullover A

STRIPES FOR SWEATER B (MULTI-STRIPED)

① With color A, knit 1 round.

② Change to color B and knit 2 rounds.
Change to color C and knit 4 rounds.
Change to color D and knit 2 rounds.
Change to color E and knit 4 rounds.
Change to color A and knit 2 rounds.

③ Work the stripe pattern shown in Step 2 until the body measures 7½ (9, 10½) inches, then go to the "Back" section on the next page.

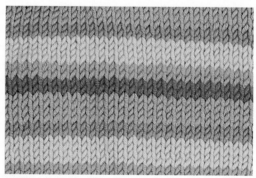

Striped Pullover B

BACK

1 Continuing in color A for Sweater A, or in the established stripe pattern for Sweater B, knit across the first 64 (70, 74) stitches for the back. Slip the remaining 64 (70, 74) front stitches to a stitch holder or piece of waste yarn. You will work the remainder of the body back and forth in rows.

2 Turn your work so that the wrong side is facing you and purl across the back stitches.

3 Continue to work back and forth in stockinette stitch on the back stitches in color A or the established stripe pattern until the back measures 14 (16, 18) inches from the cast-on edge. End having completed a wrong-side row. Slip these stitches to a stitch holder or piece of waste yarn. Cut yarn, leaving a 10-inch tail.

FRONT

1 Transfer the front stitches to the circular needle. Continuing in color A or the established stripe pattern, attach a new ball of yarn to the right edge of the front and knit across the 64 (70, 74) front stitches. Turn your work so that the wrong side is facing you and purl across the front stitches.

2 Continue to work back and forth in stockinette on the front stitches in color A or the established stripe pattern until the front measures 12 (14, 16) inches from the cast-on edge. End having completed a wrong-side row.

3 Continuing in color A or the established stripe pattern, knit 26 (28, 29) stitches for the left shoulder, bind off the center 12 (14, 16) stitches, and knit the next 26 (28, 29) stitches for the right shoulder. Turn. You will now work the left and right front shoulders separately.

RIGHT FRONT SHOULDER

1 (WS) Purl to end of row. Turn.

2 (RS) K1, ssk, knit to end of row. Turn.

3 Repeat steps 1–2, 6 more times—19 (21, 22) stitches remain on right shoulder.

4 Work even (without decreasing) until the right shoulder measures 14 (16, 18) inches from the cast-on edge. End having completed a wrong-side row. Then slip the stitches to a stitch holder or piece of waste yarn. Cut yarn, leaving a 10-inch tail.

Decreases in neck

LEFT FRONT SHOULDER

❶ (WS) Attach yarn to the inside neck edge of the left shoulder and purl to the end of the row. Turn.

❷ (RS) Knit to the last 3 stitches, k2tog, k1. Turn.

❸ Repeat steps 1–2, 6 more times—19 (21, 22) stitches remain on left shoulder.

❹ Work even (without increasing) until the right shoulder measures 14 (16, 18) inches from the cast-on edge. End having completed a wrong-side row. Transfer these stitches to a double-pointed needle. Do not cut yarn.

JOIN THE SHOULDERS

❶ Transfer the back stitches to the circular needle. Turn the sweater inside out and arrange the right and left front shoulder stitches so that they are properly aligned with the back stitches.

❷ Using the yarn still attached to the left front shoulder, work a three-needle bind-off (see page 236) to join the first 19 (21, 22) back stitches to the 19 (21, 22) left front shoulder stitches.

❸ Bind off the next 26 (28, 30) stitches for the back of the neck.

❹ Transfer the right front shoulder stitches to a double-pointed needle. Use the three-needle bind-off to join the remaining 19 (21, 22) back stitches to the right front shoulder stitches.

❺ Turn the work right side out. Cut yarn, leaving a 10-inch tail.

Front/back shoulder join of Striped Pullover B

SLEEVES

❶ Using the double-pointed needles and color A, pick up and knit 68 (72, 78) stitches evenly around one of the armholes, beginning at the underarm. Join to work in the round, placing a marker to indicate the end of the round.

❷ Knit 1 round.

Where sleeve meets body of Striped Pullover A

③ Begin shaping the sleeve as described below, while working the following stripe pattern:

For Sweater A: Knit 16 rounds in color B, then work the remainder of the sleeve in color A.

For Sweater B: Work the established stripe pattern *in reverse* (4 rounds E, 2 rounds D, 4 rounds C, 2 rounds B, 2 rounds A).

④ K1, ssk, knit to 3 stitches before the marker, k2tog, k1—2 stitches decreased.

⑤ Knit 3 rounds.

⑥ Repeat steps 4–5, 15 (17, 18) more times—36 (36, 40) stitches remain.

⑦ Work even (without decreasing) until the sleeve measures 11 (11¾, 13½) inches or desired length to ribbing.

⑧ Change to color A and work in knit 2, purl 2 rib for 1½ (2, 2) inches.

⑨ Bind off loosely in pattern.

⑩ Repeat steps 1–9 to make the second sleeve.

Cuff of Striped Pullover A

NECKBAND

① With the right side of the work facing, use the double-pointed needles and color A to pick up and knit 26 (28, 30) stitches across the back neck, 15 stitches from the left neck edge, 12 (14, 16) stitches from the front neck edge, and 15 stitches from the right neck edge—68 (72, 76) stitches total. Join to work in the round, placing a marker to indicate the end of the round.

② Work in knit 2, purl 2 rib for 1½ inches.

③ Bind off very loosely in pattern.

Neckband of Striped Pullover A

FINISHING

① Weave in yarn tails.

② Wash and block the sweater if desired.

Adult's Center-Cable Pullover

Perfect on just about everyone, this simple pullover with its centered cable is a sweater you'll reach for again and again. There's waist shaping to accent feminine curves, or leave out the shaping for a looser-fitting sweater more appropriate for your favorite guy.

Center-Cable Pullover A

Center-Cable Pullover B

Specifications

SIZE
Chest circumference: 36 (40, 44, 48, 52) inches

YARN
1300 (1690, 2080, 2425, 2740) yards of DK-weight yarn

Sweater A: Foxfire *Cormo Silk Alpaca* (55% fine Cormo wool/25% bombyx silk/20% prime alpaca, 190 yd. per skein), 7 (9, 11, 13, 15) skeins in color Juniper

Sweater B: Berroco *Ultra Alpaca* (50% super-fine alpaca/50% Peruvian wool, 215 yd. per skein), 6 (8, 10, 12, 13) skeins in color Candied Yam Mix

NEEDLES
US 5 32-inch circular needle, or size needed to obtain gauge

Set of 4 or 5 US 5 double-pointed needles (If you prefer, you can work the sleeves on a second 32-inch circular using the magic-loop method instead.)

US 5 16-inch circular needle

(The length and type of needles required will vary depending on the circular knitting method you use. See the "Plan the Pullover" section on the next page for details.)

NOTIONS
Stitch markers
Cable needle
Stitch holders or waste yarn
Seaming needle

GAUGE
5½ stitches × 7 rows per inch, in stockinette stitch worked in the round

Plan the Pullover

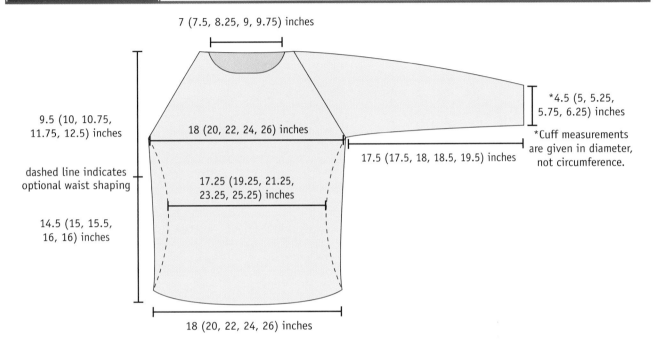

7 (7.5, 8.25, 9, 9.75) inches

9.5 (10, 10.75, 11.75, 12.5) inches

*4.5 (5, 5.25, 5.75, 6.25) inches

18 (20, 22, 24, 26) inches

*Cuff measurements are given in diameter, not circumference.

dashed line indicates optional waist shaping

17.5 (17.5, 18, 18.5, 19.5) inches

17.25 (19.25, 21.25, 23.25, 25.25) inches

14.5 (15, 15.5, 16, 16) inches

18 (20, 22, 24, 26) inches

CONSTRUCTION OVERVIEW
You work this garment entirely in the round. Beginning at the hem, you work the body from the bottom up. You work sleeves separately in the round, then join them to the body at the underarm. You gradually decrease the sleeves and body as you work the yoke. These decreases, called *raglan decreases*, form diagonal lines running from the underarm to the neck. Then you work the neckband from stitches picked up around the neckline. "Seaming" takes place only when joining the underarm stitches of the body.

CIRCULAR KNITTING METHOD
You can work the body of this sweater in the traditional method on a 32-inch circular needle. You can start the sleeves on double-pointed needles and move them to a 16-inch circular when there are enough stitches to fit around the needle. You can pick up the neckband and work it on a 16-inch circular needle.

YARN SELECTION
When choosing yarn for this project, consider both the weight of the yarn and its ability to show stitches clearly (called *stitch definition*). Plied yarns tend to give greater stitch definition than single-ply yarns. Yarns that exhibit a halo, such as angora and mohair, are not recommended, as these yarns tend to blur stitches together. Also, select a yarn that is dyed in a solid, semi solid, or heather color. Variegated or striping yarns will obscure the cable pattern.

Stitch Pattern

CENTER CABLE

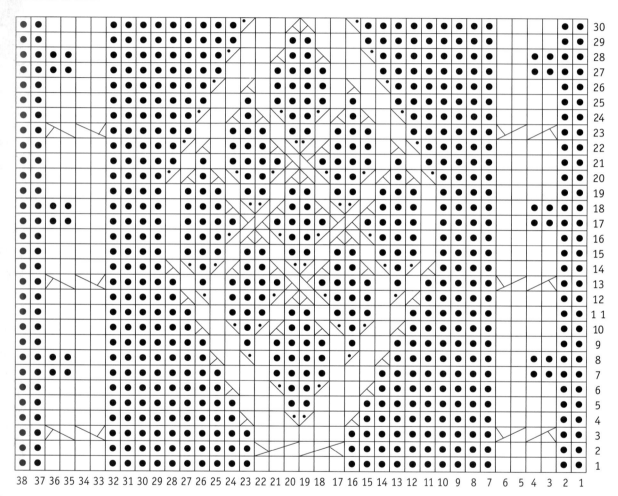

NOTE: This chart will be worked mainly in the round using the RS directions. The WS instructions will only be needed when working the pattern back and forth during the neck shaping.

Key

RS: Purl
WS: Knit

RS: Knit
WS: Purl

C3/3R (cable 3 over 3 right)
RS: Slip 3 sts to cable needle and hold in back, k3, k3 from cable needle.
WS: Slip 3 sts to cable needle and hold in back, p3, p3 from cable needle.

C2/2R (cable 2 over 2 right)
RS: Slip 2 sts to cable needle and hold in back, k2, k2 from cable needle.
WS: Slip 2 sts to cable needle and hold in back, p2, p2 from cable needle.

C2/2L (cable 2 over 2 left)
RS: Slip 2 sts to cable needle and hold in front, k2, k2 from cable needle.
WS: Slip 2 sts to cable needle and hold in front, p2, p2 from cable needle.

C3/1PR (cable 3 over 1 purl right)
RS: Slip 1 st to cable needle and hold in back, k3, p1 from cable needle.
WS: Slip 3 sts to cable needle and hold in back, k1, p3 from cable needle.

C3/1PL (cable 3 over 1 purl left)
RS: Slip 3 sts to cable needle and hold in front, p1, k3 from cable needle.
WS: Slip 1 st to cable needle and hold in front, p3, k1 from cable needle.

C2/1PR (cable 2 over 1 purl right)
RS: Slip 1 st to cable needle and hold in back, k2, p1 from cable needle.
WS: Slip 2 sts to cable needle and hold in back, k1, p2 from cable needle.

C2/1PL (cable 2 over 1 purl left)
RS: Slip 2 sts to cable needle and hold in front, p1, k2 from cable needle.
WS: Slip 1 st to cable needle and hold in front, p2, k1 from cable needle.

C1/1PL (cable 1 over 1 purl left)
RS/WS: Slip 1 st to cable needle and hold in front, p1, k1 from cable needle.

C1/1PR (cable 1 over 1 purl right)
RS/WS: Slip 1 st to cable needle and hold in back, k1, p1 from cable needle.

C1/1L (cable 1 over 1 left)
RS: Slip 1 st to cable needle and hold in front, k1, k1 from cable needle.
WS: Slip 1 st to cable needle and hold in front, p1, p1 from cable needle.

C1/1R (cable 1 over 1 right)
RS: Slip 1 st to cable needle and hold in back, k1, k1 from cable needle.
WS: Slip 1 st to cable needle and hold in back, p1, p1 from cable needle.

Make the Pullover

BODY

1 Using the 32-inch circular needle, cast on 212 (236, 256, 280, 300) stitches using the long-tail cast-on (see page 28). Join for working in the round, being careful not to twist your cast on around the needles. Place a marker to indicate the end of the round.

2 Knit 106 (118, 128, 140, 150) stitches, then place a marker to identify the side of the pullover. Knit to the end of the round.

3 Knit until the work measures 1½ inches from the cast-on edge.

4 Purl 1 round to create a turning ridge for the hem.

5 *Knit 34 (40, 45, 51, 56) stitches, work row 1 of the cable chart (38 stitches), knit 34 (40, 45, 51, 56) stitches, slip marker; repeat from * once.

6 Continue as established, working the center 38 stitches on the front and back according to the cable chart and knitting all other stitches, until the work measures 4 (4¼, 4½, 4¾, 4¾) inches from the purled turning ridge.

Center cable panel

WAIST SHAPING (OPTIONAL)

Waist shaping adds a feminine touch to a woman's sweater. If you're making a man's sweater, skip to the "Middle Body" section.

1 *K1, ssk, work in pattern as established to 3 stitches before the side marker, k2tog, k1, slip marker; repeat from * once—4 stitches decreased.

Waist-shaping

② Work 7 rounds even (without decreasing), then repeat Step 1 once more—204 (228, 248, 272, 292) stitches total.

③ Work even until the body measures 9½ (9¾, 10, 10¼, 10¼) inches from the purled turning ridge.

④ Reverse the waist shaping as follows. *K1, make 1, work in pattern as established to 1 stitch before marker, make 1, k1, slip marker; repeat from * once—4 stitches increased.

⑤ Work 7 rounds even, then repeat Step 4 once more—212 (236, 256, 280, 300) stitches total.

MIDDLE BODY

① Work until the body measures 14½ (15, 15½, 16, 16) inches or the desired length from the purled turning ridge.

② Set the body aside, leaving it on the circular needle. You will join the sleeves to the body when they are complete.

SLEEVES

① Using the double-pointed needles, cast on 50 (54, 58, 64, 70) stitches using the long-tail cast on. Join for working in the round, being sure not to twist the cast on around the needles. Place a marker to indicate the end of the round.

② Knit all rounds until the work measures 1½ inches from the cast-on edge.

③ Purl 1 round to create a turning ridge for the hem.

④ Knit all rounds until the work measures 1½ inches from the purled turning ridge.

Cuff

5 K1, make 1, knit to 1 stitch before the marker, make 1, k1—2 stitches increased.

6 Knit 8 (7, 7, 6, 6) rounds.

7 Repeat steps 5–6, 10 (12, 13, 14, 14) more times—72 (80, 86, 94, 100) stitches total. Change to the 16-inch circular when you have enough stitches to fit around the needle.

8 Work even (without increasing) until the sleeve measures 17½ (17½, 18, 18½, 19½) inches or the desired length from the purled turning ridge.

Increases along sleeve length

9 Cut yarn, leaving an extra-long 24-inch tail.

10 Slip the sleeve stitches onto a piece of waste yarn and set aside. Repeat steps 1–9 to create a second sleeve. Leave the second sleeve on the needle.

JOIN SLEEVES TO BODY

1 Return to the body and work in pattern as established to 5 (6, 7, 8, 8) stitches before the side marker. Thread a 12-inch length of waste yarn onto a seaming needle and slip the next 10 (12, 14, 16, 16) body stitches onto it. Set the body aside temporarily.

2 Take the sleeve that is still on the 16-inch circular needle and, using the long tail of sleeve yarn, knit the first 5 (6, 7, 8, 8) stitches of the sleeve. Then take another piece of waste yarn and slip onto it the first 10 (12, 14, 16, 16) stitches on the right-hand needle (the 5[6,7,8,8] stitches just worked plus the last 5 [6, 7, 8, 8] stitches of the previous round).

3 Using the body needle and the body yarn, knit the remaining 62 (68, 72, 78, 84) sleeve stitches.

4 Continuing with the body needle, work across the back of the sweater in the established pattern to 5 (6, 7, 8, 8) stitches before the end of the round. Slip the next 5 (6, 7, 8, 8) stitches onto another piece of waste yarn, remove the end-of-round marker, and slip the next 5 (6, 7, 8, 8) stitches onto the same waste yarn. Set the body aside temporarily.

5 Take the sleeve that is still on waste yarn and transfer the stitches to the 16-inch circular needle. Then repeat steps 2–3 to attach this sleeve to the body. Both sleeves are now joined to the body—316 (348, 372, 404, 436) total stitches.

YOKE

1 Work in pattern across the first 67 (72, 76, 81, 86) stitches of the front to the end of the cable panel, then place a marker to indicate the new end of the round.

2 Work 1 round while placing markers as follows: Knit the remaining 29 (34, 38, 43, 48) stitches of the front, place marker, knit 62 (68, 72, 78, 84) stitches for the right sleeve, place marker, work 96 (106, 114, 124, 134) stitches in the established pattern for the back, place marker, knit 62 (68, 72, 78, 84) stitches for the left sleeve, place marker, work in pattern to the end of the round.

Raglan area

3 Continue as established, working the center panels in pattern and keeping all other stitches in stockinette stitch, for another 1¼ (1, 1¼, 1¼, 1¼) inches.

4 Create the raglan decreases as follows: Knit to 2 stitches before marker, ssk, slip marker, k2tog, knit across right sleeve to 2 stitches before marker, ssk, slip marker, k2tog, work in pattern across the back to 2 stitches before marker, ssk, slip marker, k2tog, knit across left sleeve to 2 stitches before marker, ssk, slip marker, k2tog, work in pattern to the end of the round—8 stitches decreased.

5 Work 1 round in the established pattern without decreasing.

6 Repeat steps 4–5, 22 (25, 27, 30, 33) more times, ending after having worked the last decrease round (Step 4). 132 (140, 148, 156, 164) total stitches remain, with 16 stitches for each sleeve and 50 (54, 58, 62, 66) stitches each for the front and back.

NECKLINE SHAPING

1 Work in pattern without decreasing to the end of the left sleeve (the 4th marker). Then work the first 15 stitches of the front in pattern, and bind off the next 20 (24, 28, 32, 36) stitches for the center front neck.

2 For the remainder of the neck shaping, you work the sweater back and forth in rows; the stitch on the right-hand needle (from the bind-off) counts as the first stitch of the row. Continue the raglan decreases and begin decreasing at each side of the neck as follows: ssk, work in established pattern to 2 stitches before the right sleeve marker, ssk, slip marker, k2tog. Continue to work raglan decreases in pattern to the last 3 stitches of the row, k2tog, k1. Turn.

Decreases along side of neck

3 (WS) Work in pattern to the end of the row without decreasing. Turn.

4 (RS) K1, ssk, work to 2 stitches before the marker, work the raglan decreases as usual, continue as established to last 3 stitches of the row, k2tog, k1. Turn.

5 Repeat steps 3–4, 4 more times—52 (56, 60, 64, 68) total stitches remain, with 38 (42, 46, 50, 54) stitches for the back neck, 4 for each sleeve, and 3 for each side of the front neck.

6 Work one more wrong-side row. Turn. Then bind off all stitches.

NECKBAND

You work the neckband in the round with stitches that you pick up around the neck edge.

1 Using the 16-inch circular needle, with right side facing, pick up and knit 38 (42, 46, 50, 54) stitches across the back neck, 4 stitches across the left sleeve, 15 stitches across the left neck edge, 20 (24, 28, 32, 36) stitches across the center front neck, 15 stitches across the right neck edge, and 4 stitches across the right sleeve—96 (104, 112, 120, 128) stitches total. Join to work in the round, placing a marker to indicate the end of the round.

Ribbed neckband

2 Work in knit 2, purl 2 rib until the neckband measures 1½ inches.

3 Bind off loosely in pattern.

FINISHING

1 Finish the right armhole as follows: Transfer each set of 10 (12, 14, 16, 16) stitches at the right underarm from waste yarn to a separate needle. (You can use dpns or the two ends of one circular needle.) Hold these two needles together, thread the sleeve yarn tail onto a seaming needle, and work the Kitchener stitch (see page 237) to close the underarm opening. Repeat for the other armhole.

Underarm seam

2 Finish the hem as follows: Turn the sweater inside out, then fold the bottom of the sweater up along the turning ridge so that the wrong sides of the hem are together. Loosely and carefully sew the hem into place using the whipstitch (see page 238). Repeat for the hem at the bottom of each sleeve.

3 Weave in all yarn tails.

4 Wash and block the sweater, if desired.

Hem

CHAPTER 9

Steeked Projects

A little more complicated but well worth it, these projects involve cutting into your knitting to create in one instance a shawl and in the other a cardigan. The tradition of cutting into your knitting goes far back in knitting lore. With the advent of acrylic fibers and slippery, soft engineered yarns, steeking fell by the wayside. Yet this wonderful technique saves time and effort in construction and is an excellent tool to add to your knitting arsenal.

Steeks

Steeks are extra stitches knit into a circular garment that act as a bridge. They are later cut open for armholes, front openings, or neck openings, and the like. Historically they were most often used in colorwork sweaters, where tracking a pattern and changing colors is easier when the right side always faces you. However, you can use steeks in many different projects.

ABOUT STEEKS

The benefits of steeking are similar to the benefits of circular knitting: Stitch patterns are easier to knit from the right side. With no wrong-side rows, there is no need to purl your stitches unless your stitch pattern calls for them. Steeks also eliminate the need for seaming pieces together.

Many knitters are fearful when cutting their first steeks. Yet knitters have been performing this bit of magic on their work for a very long time. Learn how to create a steek and how to treat that steek before and after cutting it open, and you will cut into your projects with confidence.

YARN FOR STEEKING

When creating a knitted item with steeks, it is best to use a yarn that is 100-percent wool; Shetland wool yarns are ideal for steeking. With careful steek preparation, you can use softer yarns such as alpaca, although it is best if they are combined with wool. Acrylic, cotton, silk, and other slippery fibers are poor choices because these yarns are difficult to stabilize. The best yarns for steeking are "toothy" yarns, meaning that the fibers interlock easily, preventing your stitches from unraveling when you cut the steek.

As a general rule, if the fiber feels slippery and very soft in your hand, it is probably not a great candidate for steeking unless you take significant care to reinforce the steeks before cutting.

When planning a project, always create a test steek on a swatch made of the intended yarn to determine whether it is appropriate for the project.

Toothy yarns—good for steeking

Smooth yarns—bad for steeking

How to Create a Steek

KNIT A STEEK

To create a steek, you cast on extra stitches (usually between 3 and 10) for each steek in your garment and set them off from the rest of your project with markers. When knitting your project, simply work the steek stitches in stockinette stitch. If you are working a colorwork project in which you are stranding two colors, work the steek stitches in a 1 × 1 checkerboard or one-column-wide stripes.

If you are creating a steek over the armhole, you first bind off the stitches at the bottom of the armhole and then, on the next round, cast on extra steek stitches to span this distance.

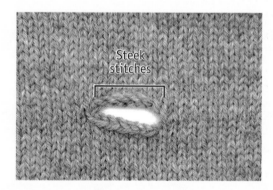

Steek stitches

PREPARE A STEEK

Before you cut open a steek, it is usually a good idea to reinforce the edges. Shetland wool and other toothy, woolen-spun yarns may not require this preparation.

① Locate the center of the steek. If your steek has an even number of stitches, this is the line between the two center columns of stitches. If your steek has an odd number of stitches as shown, this is an imaginary line running down the center column.

② Identify the column of stitches that is 1 stitch to the left and the column of stitches that is 1 stitch to the right of this imaginary center line. I will call these two columns the *boundary stitch columns*.

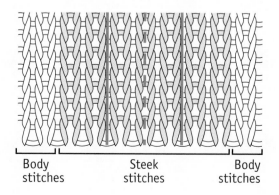

Body stitches Steek stitches Body stitches

Steek center (red dotted line) and boundary stitch columns (red lines right and left of dotted line)

195

REINFORCE A STEEK

One way to reinforce a steek is to machine stitch along the two boundary stitch columns of stitches. You can also reinforce the steek by hand, backstitching with a contrasting color of thread (for better visibility). For large steeks, it is quicker to machine stitch. Set the machine to sew a straight seam. Be aware that machine-sewn steeks can be somewhat rigid; make a test swatch before using this method with a smaller armhole to avoid an uncomfortable sleeve fit.

A machine-sewn steek

Another way to reinforce a steek is to work a crochet chain along both of the boundary stitch columns. A crocheted edge will tighten the underlying stitches, making it harder for them to unravel. This can even be a decorative touch to the inside of a garment if you work it in a coordinating color.

Steek with a crocheted edge

TIP

If you are using a sewing machine, it may be helpful to place scraps of paper on top of your knitted piece to prevent the presser foot of the sewing machine from catching on your work, and beneath it to keep the yarn from being forced into the bobbin of the machine. You can simply tear the paper away once the machine stitching is in place.

CUT A STEEK

Using a sharp pair of small scissors, cut down the center of the steek between the two columns of stitching you have made. Be careful not to cut through any steek-reinforcing stitches.

NOTE: You may notice that although vigorous tugging releases the stitches, average tugs do not. When you knit the stitches in toothy wool yarns, they are not in any hurry to escape. This can give you confidence that your steeks will stand up to daily use when you incorporate them into a garment.

Cutting steek with sharp scissors

PICK UP STITCHES ALONG A CUT STEEK

Pick up and knit along the edge of the steek, picking up one stitch over from the actual steek stitches (see illustration). This means that you are picking up and knitting into body stitches, not steek stitches. Your pattern will tell you how many stitches to pick up around an armhole or around a neck opening to create a neckband.

NOTE: In the figure at right, stitches should be picked up and knit along the yellow stitch line.

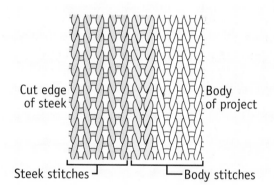

Cut edge of steek   Body of project

Steek stitches   Body stitches

COVER A CUT STEEK

On the wrong side of your steeked project, you will notice messy ends where you cut the steek. In the case of a garment made from a toothy wool, you can leave the fibers from the cut ends alone and they will gradually felt and mat together with the garment. If this option does not appeal to you, you can fold back the steek against the wrong side of the garment and tuck under the cut ends of the steek. You can then whipstitch the folded steek down on the wrong side of the garment using your project yarn and a seaming needle.

Messy ends on wrong side of steeked swatch

Whipstitching a folded-under steek

Simple Steeked Shawl

This shawl is an excellent way to practice steeking with minimal commitment and very little fear. I got the idea for this project when I discovered a bright-orange scarf in the yarn stash giveaway of the talented Kirsten Hipsky. It was worked in a simple trellis lace pattern from Barbara Walker's **A Treasury of Knitting Patterns.** Kirsten worked her version back and forth, but I have adapted it to be worked in the round with a steek that creates the fringe. (See photos on pages 198 and 199 for Shawl A and three variations.)

Shawl A

Specifications

SIZE

This shawl is shaped like a parallelogram. You can make it to any desired length and width. The length is determined by the number of stitches you cast on; the width is determined by how far you knit before you bind off. You can also work the project as a scarf by knitting less width. See below for the dimensions of the shawls and scarves pictured here.

NOTE: The length of the shawls and scarves does not include the fringe.

Shawl B

Shawl A: Valley Yarns *Goshen* (48% Peruvian cotton/46% modal/6% silk, 92 yd. per ball), 7 balls in color Sage. This shawl was worked at a gauge of 3 stitches per inch (in pattern) and measures approximately 72 × 18 inches.

Shawl B: Spirit Trail Fiberworks *Penelope* (50% bombyx silk/50% merino, 437 yd. per skein), 2 skeins in color River's Edge. This shawl was worked at a gauge of 5 stitches per inch (in pattern) and measures approximately 60 × 16 inches.

Scarf C: Lorna's Laces *Pearl* (51% silk/49% bamboo, 220 yd. per skein), 1 skein in color 308 Huron. This scarf was worked at a gauge of 4 stitches per inch (in pattern) and measures approximately 72 × 4 inches.

Scarf D: Blue Moon Fiber Arts *Luscious Silk* (100% silk, 360 yd. per skein), 1 skein in color Backstabber. This scarf was worked at a gauge of 4 stitches per inch (in pattern) and measures approximately 72 × 6 inches.

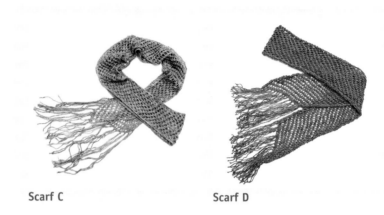

Scarf C   Scarf D

YARN

You can use virtually any weight of yarn for this project. See "Yarn Selection" on page 201 for recommendations. The number of yards you need will vary, depending on your gauge as well as the length and width of your shawl. The table below will give you a rough estimate of the yardage you may need.

Approximate Yardages for 50–72" × 18" Shawl	
Gauge in Pattern Stitch	Approximate Yardage
3 stitches/inch	510–755 yards
4 stitches/inch	850–1220 yards
5 stitches/inch	990–1420 yards
6 stitches/inch	1085–1565 yards
7 stitches/inch	1195–1720 yards

NEEDLES

One 32-inch (or longer) circular needle in the size needed to get your desired gauge

NOTIONS

Pair of sharp scissors
Stitch markers

GAUGE

Gauge is less important here than with any other project in this book, but the table at the top of the next page will give you an idea of how many stitches to cast on to achieve a particular finished length. Swatch in the pattern stitch to determine the number of pattern stitches to cast on for the correct size of your finished project. You will cast on extra stitches for the fringe: an additional 30 stitches for a gauge of 3 to 5 stitches per inch and an additional 50 stitches for a gauge of 6 to 7 stitches per inch.

NOTE: Due to the method in which this shawl is constructed, the fringe is an integral part of the project and cannot be left out.

The number of stitches cast on in the table at right are all multiples of 2. If you decide to vary your number of cast-on stitches from those given above but still wish to use the Trellis Lace pattern below, remember to cast on a number of pattern stitches that is divisible by 2.

Number of Stitches to Cast On					
Desired Length	**50"**	**56"**	**60"**	**66"**	**72"**
Gauge in Pattern Stitch					
3 stitches/inch	150	168	180	198	216
4 stitches/inch	200	224	240	264	288
5 stitches/inch	250	280	300	330	360
6 stitches/inch	300	336	360	396	432
7 stitches/inch	350	392	420	462	504

Stitch Pattern

TRELLIS LACE STITCH (MULTIPLE OF 2 STITCHES)

① Round 1: *Yo, k2tog; repeat from * to end of round.

② Round 2: Knit.

Plan the Shawl

Shawl B

CONSTRUCTION OVERVIEW

This project is worked in the round lengthwise, so the number of stitches that you cast on determines the length of the shawl. You will cast on extra stitches for the fringe, which you will work as a steek. You will work the project in the round to the desired width. Then you cut the steek open and unravel it to create a fringe that hangs from each end of the shawl.

CIRCULAR KNITTING METHOD

Because of the large circumference of this project, it is best to work with one circular needle in the traditional method. Use a circular that can accommodate all of the stitches for your shawl (generally not less than 32 inches). See Chapter 2 for information on choosing needles for this method.

YARN SELECTION

In general, when working steeks it is advisable to choose a yarn that is not slippery and has a lot of wool or other toothy fiber in it. However, because the steeks in this project are unraveled and knotted, your yarn choices are limitless. Choose a shiny, luxuriant yarn in a lighter weight for an evening shawl or a soft, warm wool yarn in a heavier weight for a winter scarf. Variegated yarns, such as the one used for Shawl B, are perfect for this project. A more complicated lace pattern would be obscured by the color changes in a yarn of this type, but this simple lace pattern allows the colors to shine. Also, the holes in the lace pattern break up any pooling that might otherwise occur with a variegated yarn.

Variegated color—Shawl B

Feel free to replace the simple lace pattern presented here with one of those included in Chapter 10. Be sure to knit a swatch of any stitch pattern you are considering. Then evaluate both the right and wrong sides of the pattern, as both will be visible in the completed project.

Make the Shawl

1. Using the backward-loop cast-on (see page 234), cast on an even number of stitches from the chart on the previous page. Cast on an additional 30–50 stitches for the fringe. Join to work in the round, being careful not to twist the cast-on around the needle. Place a marker to indicate the end of the round.

2. Knit the number of stitches that you cast on for the fringe, place a marker to indicate the end of the fringe, and knit to the end of the round.

3 Knit to the marker, slip marker, *yo, k2tog; repeat from * to the end of the round.

4 Knit 1 round.

5 Repeat steps 3 and 4 until the shawl is the desired width, measured from the cast-on edge. End having just completed a yarn-over round.

NOTE: A width of 16–24 inches makes a comfortable shawl. For a scarf, a width of 4–10 inches is more typical.

6 Knit to the marker, slip marker, and then bind off the remaining stitches very loosely to the end of the round (do not bind off any of the fringe stitches at the beginning of the next round). Cut the yarn, leaving a 12-inch tail. Pull up on the loop remaining from the bind-off until the yarn tail comes free and the loop no longer remains.

7 Slide the fringe stitches off the needle and unravel them all the way down to the cast-on edge.

8 Cut the unraveled strands in the middle to create fringe. Tie the fringe, including the tails from your cast on and bind-off, in overhand knots in groups of 3 or 4 strands. Before tightening each knot, slide it up so that it is snug against the body of the shawl.

9 Trim the ends of the fringe to your desired length.

10 Wash the shawl and block it by laying it flat to dry.

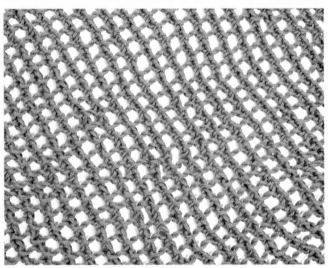

Close-up of stitch pattern—Shawl A

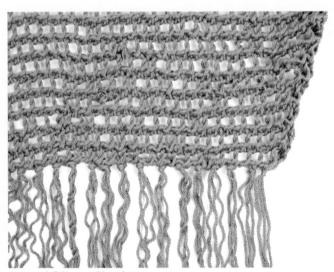

Knotted fringe—Shawl A

I love cardigans, and I love steeks. This sweater gives me the best of both worlds: a simple and comfortable cardigan with a shape that fits easily over my winter clothes, and the benefits of steeking and all that endless stockinette stitch that's perfect for mindless, relaxing knitting.

Specifications

SIZE
Chest circumference: 34 (38, 42, 46, 50) inches

YARN
1300 (1580, 1800, 2080, 2355) yards of worsted-weight yarn

Pictured: Spirit Trail Fiberworks *Vega* (50% fine alpaca/50% merino, 437 yards, per skein), 3 (4, 5, 5, 6) skeins in color Tierra del Mar.

NEEDLES
US 7, 32-inch circular needle, or size needed to obtain gauge
US 10, 32-inch circular needle, or 3 sizes larger than that needed to obtain gauge
US 7, 16-inch circular needle
Set of 4 or 5 US 7 double-pointed needles
Set of 4 or 5 US 10 double-pointed needles

(If you prefer, you can work the sleeves on a 32-inch circular needle using the magic loop method. See "Construction Overview" on page 204.)

NOTIONS
Stitch markers
Seaming needle
Sharp pair of scissors
Sewing needle
Sewing thread in color to match yarn
Sewing machine, if desired for reinforcing steeks
Crochet hook in size H (5mm), if desired for reinforcing steeks
2 frog closures (optional, not shown)

GAUGE
5 stitches × 7 rows per inch, worked in stockinette stitch using the smaller needle

Plan the Cardigan

CONSTRUCTION OVERVIEW

You work this cardigan completely in the round, with steeks spanning the openings for the front and the sleeves. You work the body as a tube from the hem to the shoulders, which you then join with a three-needle bind-off. After cutting open the steeks, you pick up the sleeves from around the armholes and work them in the round.

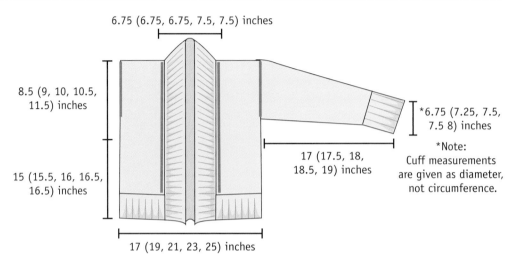

6.75 (6.75, 6.75, 7.5, 7.5) inches

8.5 (9, 10, 10.5, 11.5) inches

15 (15.5, 16, 16.5, 16.5) inches

17 (19, 21, 23, 25) inches

17 (17.5, 18, 18.5, 19) inches

*6.75 (7.25, 7.5, 7.5 8) inches

*Note: Cuff measurements are given as diameter, not circumference.

Red lines indicate locations of steeks
that are cut during finishing of garment.

CIRCULAR KNITTING METHOD

You can work the body of this sweater with a 32-inch circular needle in the traditional method. You can work the sleeves with a 16-inch circular until there are too few stitches to fit around the needle, and then finish the sleeves on double-pointed needles. My preferred method is to work the body on a 32-inch circular, but to use the same magic-loop style to work the entire length of the sleeves. See Chapter 2 for more information about different methods of circular knitting.

NOTE: With either method, you work the ribbed portions of the cardigan on a needle that is three sizes larger than the needle that you use for the stockinette portions.

YARN SELECTION

Choosing yarn for this project is very important because it will be steeked. Some yarns are better suited to this technique than others; see "Yarn for Steeking" on page 194 for details.

For the cardigan pictured here, I chose a yarn that would not traditionally be used for steeking. I fell in love with the beautifully blended hues of this peaceful colorway. As a result, I chose to use a method for steek finishing that locks the slippery alpaca fibers into place to prevent unraveling.

Knit the Cardigan

BODY

1 With the larger 32-inch circular needle, cast on 146 (166, 186, 202, 222) stitches. Join to work in the round, being careful not to twist the cast-on around the needle. Place a marker to indicate the end of the round.

NOTE: The end of the round is at the front of the cardigan, at the beginning of an 8-stitch-wide steek.

2 Knit 8 stitches and place a marker to indicate the end of the front steek. Then work to the end of the round in knit 2, purl 2 rib, ending with a knit 2.

3 Continue working in the round as established, knitting the first 8 stitches for the front steek and then working the remaining stitches in knit 2, purl 2 rib, until the piece measures 3½ inches from the cast-on edge.

4 Change to the smaller 32-inch circular needle and work in stockinette stitch until the piece measures 15 (15½, 16, 16½, 16½) inches from the cast-on edge.

5 Knit the 8 stitches of the front steek, then the 21 (26, 31, 34, 37) stitches of the right front. Bind off the next 10 (10, 10, 10, 14) stitches for the right armhole. Knit across the next 76 (86, 96, 106, 112) stitches for the back. Bind off 10 (10, 10, 10, 14) stitches for the left armhole. Knit across 21 (26, 31, 34, 37) stitches for the left front.

6 Create steeks for the sleeves by casting on stitches over the places where you bound off stitches on the previous round, as follows: knit to the first bind-off. Using the backward-loop cast-on (see page 234), cast on 8 stitches for the right armhole steek. Knit to the second bind-off, cast-on another 8 stitches for the left armhole steek, and knit to the end of the round.

7 Work in stockinette stitch until the piece measures 23½ (24½, 26, 27, 28) inches from the cast-on edge.

8 Bind off the first 8 stitches (the front steek). Knit across the next 21 (26, 31, 34, 37) stitches for the right front shoulder. Bind off the 8 steek stitches for the right armhole. Knit across 21 (26, 31, 34, 37) stitches for the right back shoulder. Bind off 34 (34, 34, 38, 38) stitches for the back neck. Knit across 21 (26, 31, 34, 37) stitches for the left back shoulder. Bind off the 8 steek stitches for the left armhole. Knit across 21 (26, 31, 34, 37) stitches for the left front shoulder.

⑨ Turn the work inside out. Transfer the left front shoulder stitches to one small dpn and the left back shoulder stitches to another dpn. Use a three-needle bind-off (see page 236) to join these 2 sets of stitches. Repeat for the right shoulder. Turn the work right side out.

CUT STEEKS

① Reinforce the front and armhole steeks using one of the methods described on page 196.

② Cut open each steek.

SLEEVES

① Using the 16-inch circular needle, pick up and knit 96 (102, 110, 116, 128) stitches evenly around one of the armholes, beginning at the underarm. (See page 197 for details on picking up stitches along steeked edges.) Join to work in the round, placing a marker to indicate the end of the round.

② Work in stockinette stitch until the sleeve measures 1 (1, 1½, 1½, ½) inches from the picked-up edge.

③ K1, SSK, knit to 3 stitches before the marker, k2tog, k1—2 stitches decreased.

④ Knit 3 (3, 2, 2, 2) rounds.

⑤ Repeat steps 3–4, 13 (14, 16, 19, 23) times—68 (72, 76, 76, 80) stitches remain. Change to dpns as soon as your stitches no longer fit around the 16-inch circular needle.

⑥ Work even (without decreasing) until the sleeve measures 13½ (14, 14½, 15, 15½) inches.

Top of shoulder where front joins back

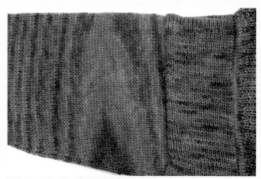

Where sleeve joins body

7 Change to the larger dpns and work in knit 2, purl 2 rib for 3½ inches.

8 Bind off loosely in pattern.

9 Repeat steps 1–8 to create the second sleeve.

FRONT BAND

1 With the right side facing and using the larger 32-inch circular needle, beginning at the lower-right edge of the cardigan's center opening, pick up and knit 124 (128, 136, 144, 148) stitches along the right front, 34 (34, 34, 38, 38) stitches along the back neck edge, and 124 (128, 136, 144, 148) stitches along the left front—282 (290, 306, 326, 338) stitches total. Turn. You work the front band back and forth in rows.

2 (WS) *Purl 2, knit 2; repeat from * to the last 2 stitches, purl 2. Turn.

3 (RS) *Knit 2, purl 2; repeat from * to the last 2 stitches, knit 2.

4 Repeat steps 2 and 3 until the front band measures 3½ inches. Bind off loosely in pattern.

FINISHING

1 Whipstitch the raw edges of each cut steek to the inside of the garment using the project yarn and a seaming needle.

2 Weave in yarn tails.

3 Wash and block, if desired.

4 (Optional) Sew purchased frog closures to the front of the cardigan where desired using the sewing thread and needle.

Cuff

Front band of cardigan

CHAPTER 10

Stitch Gallery

Once you are comfortable with the techniques in this book and with the concept of master patterns, you can have a lot of fun with your knitting by dressing up the various garments and making them your own. By using the stitch patterns presented in this dictionary, you can become your own designer. Each pattern is presented with a chart as well as written directions. The charts flow within each section from the simplest to the most difficult.

Patterns with fewer stitches in a repeat may be easier to fit into smaller projects such as mittens. Patterns with more stitches in a repeat lend themselves well to larger projects, such as cowls or sweaters. However you use them, these patterns can add texture and artistry to your work. For more information about how to include stitch patterns in your projects, see Chapter 5.

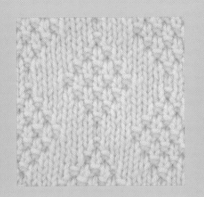

Knit and Purl Patterns

I like the arrangement of knit and purl patterns on the surface of a finished project. Not only do they add visual interest, but the varying stitches also give my hands something to do besides knit. The only two stitches involved in these patterns are the knit stitch and the purl stitch, which makes them an easy way to incorporate texture into your projects. These patterns can be an excellent introduction to working with charts, as they are simple to follow.

Knit and Purl Pattern 1 (4-Stitch Repeat)

Round 1 (RS): P1, k1, sl1, k1.

Round 2: P1, k3.

Repeat rounds 1–2 for Knit and Purl Pattern 1.

NOTE: These instructions assume you are working in the round. All rounds are worked on the right side (RS).

Key

☐ **K:** Knit

● **P:** Purl

V **Sl:** Slip 1 stitch purlwise, holding yarn in back

Knit and Purl Pattern 2 (6-Stitch Repeat)

Round 1 (RS): P1, k1, p4.

Round 2: P1, k1, p1, k3.

Round 3: P3, k3.

Round 4: P1, k1, p1, k3.

Repeat rounds 1–4 for Knit and Purl Pattern 2.

NOTE: These instructions assume you are working in the round. All rounds are worked on the right side (RS).

Key

☐ **K:** Knit

● **P:** Purl

Knit and Purl Pattern 3 (6-Stitch Repeat)

Rounds 1–3 (RS): K3, p3.

Rounds 4–6: P1, k3, p2.

Rounds 7–9: P2, k3, p1.

Rounds 10–12: P3, k3.

Rounds 13–15: K1, p3, k2.

Rounds 16–18: K2, p3, k1.

Repeat rounds 1–18 for Knit and Purl Pattern 3.

NOTE: These instructions assume you are working in the round. All rounds are worked on the right side (RS).

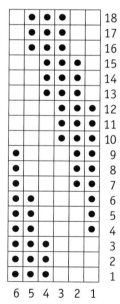

Key

☐ **K:** Knit

● **P:** Purl

Knit and Purl Pattern 4 (6-Stitch Repeat)

Rounds 1–2 (RS): K6.

Rounds 3–6: K1, p4, k1.

Rounds 7–8: K6.

Rounds 9–12: P2, k2, p2.

Repeat rounds 1–12 for Knit and Purl Pattern 4.

NOTE: These instructions assume you are working in the round. All rounds are worked on the right side (RS).

Key

☐ K: Knit

● P: Purl

Knit and Purl Pattern 5 (14-Stitch Repeat)

Rounds 1–2 (RS): (P1, k1) 4 times, k6.

Rounds 3–4: (K1, p1) 3 times, k4, p1, k3.

Rounds 5–6: K2, p1, k1, p1, k4, p1, k1, p1, k2.

Rounds 7–8: K3, p1, k4, (p1, k1) 3 times.

Rounds 9–10: K6, (k1, p1) 4 times.

Rounds 11–12: K3, p1, k4, (p1, k1) 3 times.

Rounds 13–14: K2, p1, k1, p1, k4, p1, k1, p1, k2.

Rounds 15–16: (K1, p1) 3 times, k4, p1, k3.

Repeat rounds 1–16 for Knit and Purl Pattern 5.

NOTE: These instructions assume you are working in the round. All rounds are worked on the right side (RS).

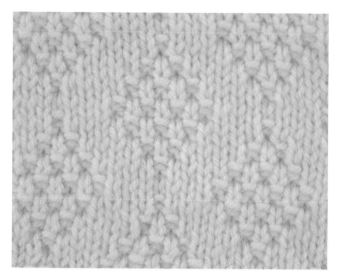

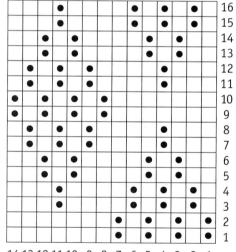

Key

☐ **K: Knit**

⬤ **P: Purl**

Knit and Purl Pattern 6 (10-Stitch Repeat)

Round 1 (RS): (P1, k1) 5 times.

Round 2: P2, (k1, p1) 3 times, k2.

Round 3: P3, (k1, p1) 2 times, k3.

Round 4: P4, k1, p1, k4.

Rounds 5–6: P5, k5.

Round 7: K1, p4, k4, p1.

Round 8: P1, k1, p3, k3, p1, k1.

Round 9: K1, p1, k1, p2, k2, p1, k1, p1.

Round 10: (P1, k1) 5 times.

Round 11: (K1, p1) 5 times.

Round 12: P1, k1, p1, k2, p2, k1, p1, k1.

Round 13: K1, p1, k3, p3, k1, p1.

Round 14: P1, k4, p4, k1.

Rounds 15–16: K5, p5.

Round 17: K4, p1, k1, p4.

Round 18: K3, (p1, k1) 2 times, p3.

Round 19: K2, (p1, k1) 3 times, p2.

Round 20: (K1, p1) 5 times.

Repeat rounds 1–20 for Knit and Purl Pattern 6.

NOTE: These instructions assume you are working in the round. All rounds are worked on the right side (RS).

Key

☐ **K:** Knit

⬛ **P:** Purl

Cable Patterns

Cables are made by removing a few stitches from your knitting needle and placing them on a cable needle, then knitting the stitches that are next in line. You then work the stitches that you held aside. In this way, you can create winding trails of raised stitches along your project. Cable patterns are a favorite of mine; I love following the path of the cables and stitches as they travel across the work.

Cable Pattern 1 (8-Stitch Repeat)

Round 1 (RS): P1, c3/3R, p1.

Rounds 2–6: P1, k6, p1.

Round 7: P1, c3/3L, p1.

Rounds 8–12: P1, k6, p1.

Repeat rounds 1–12 for Cable Pattern 1.

NOTE: These instructions assume you are working in the round. All rounds are worked on the right side (RS).

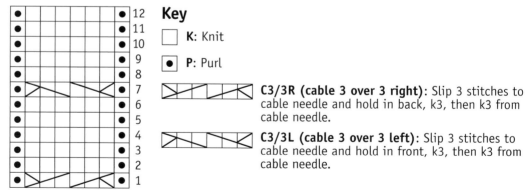

Key

☐ **K**: Knit

⏺ **P**: Purl

C3/3R (cable 3 over 3 right): Slip 3 stitches to cable needle and hold in back, k3, then k3 from cable needle.

C3/3L (cable 3 over 3 left): Slip 3 stitches to cable needle and hold in front, k3, then k3 from cable needle.

Cable Pattern 2 (8-Stitch Repeat)

Round 1 (RS): P1, k6, p1.

Round 2: P1, k2, c2/2L, p1.

Round 3: P1, k6, p1.

Round 4: P1, c2/2R, k2, p1.

Repeat rounds 1–4 for Cable Pattern 2.

NOTE: These instructions assume you are working in the round. All rounds are worked on the right side (RS).

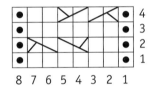

8 7 6 5 4 3 2 1

Key

 K: Knit

P: Purl

 C2/2L (cable 2 over 2 left): Slip 2 stitches to cable needle and hold in front, k2, then k2 from cable needle.

 C2/2R (cable 2 over 2 right): Slip 2 stitches to cable needle and hold in back, k2, then k2 from cable needle.

Cable Pattern 3 (12-Stitch Repeat)

Rounds 1–2 (RS): P2, k8, p2.

Round 3: P2, c2/2R, c2/2L, p2.

Rounds 4–6: P2, k8, p2.

Round 7: P2, c2/2R, c2/2L, p2.

Rounds 8–10: P2, k8, p2.

Round 11: P2, c2/2L, c2/2R, p2.

Rounds 12–14: P2, k8, p2.

Round 15: P2, c2/2L, c2/2R, p2.

Round 16: P2, k8, p2.

Repeat rounds 1–16 for Cable Pattern 3.

NOTE: These instructions assume you are working in the round. All rounds are worked on the right side (RS).

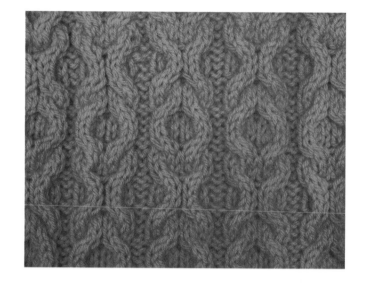

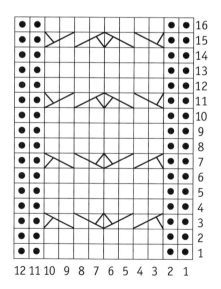

Key

☐ **K:** Knit

▣ **P:** Purl

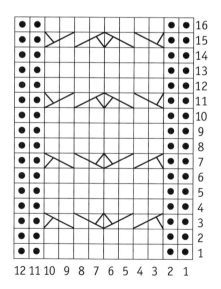 **C2/2R (cable 2 over 2 right):** Slip 2 stitches to cable needle and hold in back, k2, then k2 from cable needle.

C2/2L (cable 2 over 2 left): Slip 2 stitches to cable needle and hold in front, k2, then k2 from cable needle.

Cable Pattern 4 (10-Stitch Repeat)

Rounds 1, 3 (RS): P1, k4, (p1, k1) twice, p1.

Round 2: P1, k4, (k1, p1) twice, p1.

Round 4: P1, c4s/4R, p1.

Rounds 5, 7, 9, 11, 13: P1, (p1, k1) twice, k4, p1.

Rounds 6, 8, 10, 12: P1, (k1, p1) twice, k4, p1.

Round 14: P1, c4/4sR, p1.

Rounds 15, 17, 19: P1, k4, (p1, k1) twice, p1.

Rounds 16, 18, 20: P1, k4, (k1, p1) twice, p1.

Repeat rounds 1–20 for Cable Pattern 4.

NOTE: These instructions assume you are working in the round. All rounds are worked on the right side (RS).

Key

☐ **K**: Knit

● **P**: Purl

C4S/4R (cable 4 seed over 4 right): Slip 4 stitches to cable needle and hold in back, k1, p1, k1, p1, then k4 from cable needle.

C4/4SR (cable 4 over 4 seed right): Slip 4 stitches to cable needle and hold in back, k4, then k1, p1, k1, p1 from cable needle.

Cable Pattern 5 (12-Stitch Repeat)

Rounds 1–3 (RS): P2, k2, p4, k2, p2.

Round 4: P2, c2/2pL, c2/2pR, p2.

Round 5: P4, K4, p4.

Round 6: P4, c2/2pL, p4.

Round 7: P6, k2, p4.

Round 8: P6, c2/1pL, p3.

Round 9: P7, k2, p3.

Round 10: P7, c2/1pL, p2.

Rounds 11, 13: P8, k2, p2.

Round 12: P3, nupp, p4, k2, p2.

Round 14: P7, c2/1pR, p2.

Round 15: P7, k2, p3.

Round 16: P6, c2/1pR, p3.

Round 17: P6, k2, p4.

Round 18: P4, c2/2R, p4.

Round 19: P4, k4, p4.

Round 20: P2, c2/2pR, c2/2pL, p2.

Rounds 21–23: P2, k2, p4, k2, p2.

Round 24: P2, c2/2pL, c2/2pR, p2.

Round 25: P4, k4, p4.

Round 26: P4, c2/2pR, p4.

Round 27: P4, k2, p6.

Round 28: P3, c2/1pR, p6.

Round 29: P3, k2, p7.

Round 30: P2, c2/1pR, p7.

Rounds 31, 33: P2, k2, p8.

Round 32: P2, k2, p4, nupp, p3.

Round 34: P2, c2/1pL, p7.

Round 35: P3, k2, p7.

Round 36: P3, c2/1pL, p6.

Round 37: P4, k2, p6.

Round 38: P4, c2/2L, p4.

Round 39: P4, k4, p4.

Round 40: P2, c2/2pR, c2/2pL, p2.

Repeat rounds 1–40 for Cable Pattern 5.

NOTE: These instructions assume you are working in the round. All rounds are worked on the right side (RS).

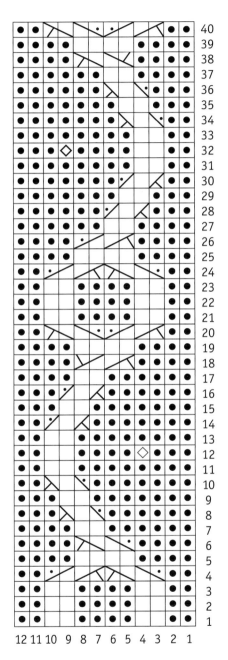

Key

☐ **K:** Knit

● **P:** Purl

◇ **Nupp:** (k1, p1, k1, p1, k1, p1, k1) in 1 stitch, pass the first 6 stitches created over the last stitch

C2/2PL (cable 2 over 2 purl left): Slip 2 stitches to cable needle and hold in front, p2, then k2 from cable.

C2/2PR (cable 2 over 2 purl right): Slip 2 stitches to cable needle and hold in back, k2, then p2 from cable.

C2/1PL (cable 2 over 1 purl left): Slip 2 stitches to cable needle and hold in front, p1, then k2 from cable.

C2/1PR (cable 2 over 1 purl right): Slip 1 stitch to cable needle and hold in back, k2, then p1 from cable.

C2/2R (cable 2 over 2 right): Slip 2 stitches to cable needle and hold in back, k2, then k2 from cable needle.

C2/2L (cable 2 over 2 left): Slip 2 stitches to cable needle and hold in front, k2, then k2 from cable needle.

Cable Pattern 6 (14-Stitch Repeat)

Rounds 1–2 (RS): P1, k12, p1.

Round 3: P1, c3/3R, c3/3L, p1.

Rounds 4–6: P1, k12, p1.

Rounds 7–8: P4, k6, p4.

Rounds 9–11: P1, k12, p1.

Round 12: P1, c3/3L, c3/3R, p1.

Rounds 13–15: P1, k12, p1.

Round 16: P1, k3, c3/3R, k3, p1.

Round 17: P1, k12, p1.

Repeat rounds 1–17 for Cable Pattern 6.

NOTE: These instructions assume you are working in the round. All rounds are worked on the right side (RS).

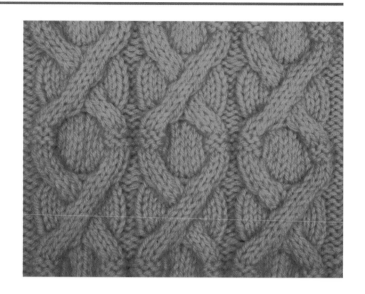

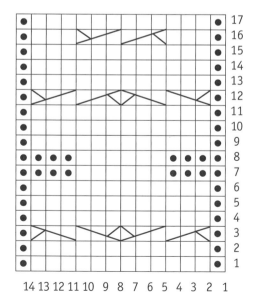

Key

☐ **K:** Knit

⬛ **P:** Purl

C3/3R (cable 3 over 3 right): Slip 3 stitches to cable needle and hold in back, k3, then k3 from cable needle.

C3/3L (cable 3 over 3 left): Slip 3 stitches to cable needle and hold in front, k3, then k3 from cable needle.

L ace is basically knitting that incorporates artfully arranged holes. You create these holes by using simple increases such as yarn overs. You then work decreases to keep the stitch count more or less constant. You can make these increases and decreases in different combinations to create a variety of effects. Lace patterns allow you to create an open, airy look in your work. For me, lace knitting is almost as enjoyable as working cables.

Lace Pattern 1 (10-Stitch Repeat)

Round 1 (RS): K1, yo, k3, cdd, k3, yo.

Round 2: K10.

Round 3: K2, yo, K2, cdd, k2, yo, k1.

Round 4: K10.

Round 5: K3, yo, k1, cdd, k1, yo, k2.

Round 6: K10.

Round 7: K4, yo, cdd, yo, k3.

Round 8: K10.

Repeat rounds 1–8 for Lace Pattern 1.

NOTE: These instructions assume you are working in the round. All rounds are worked on the right side (RS).

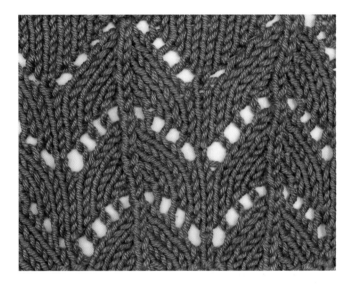

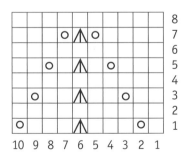

Key

☐ **K:** Knit

🔘 **Yo:** Yarn over

⋀ **Cdd (central double decrease):** Slip 2 stiches together as if to knit, k1, pass the 2 slipped stitches over the knit stitch

Lace Pattern 2 (10-Stitch Repeat)

Round 1 (RS): K2tog, yo, k6, yo, ssk.

Round 2: K10.

Round 3: K1, k2tog, yo, k4, yo, ssk, k1.

Round 4: K10.

Round 5: K2, k2tog, yo, k2, yo, ssk, k2.

Round 6: K10.

Round 7: K3, yo, ssk, k2tog, yo, k3.

Round 8: K10.

Round 9: K2, yo, ssk, k2, k2tog, yo, k2.

Round 10: K10.

Round 11: K1, yo, ssk, k4, k2tog, yo, k1.

Round 12: K10.

Repeat rounds 1–12 for Lace Pattern 2.

NOTE: These instructions assume you are working in the round. All rounds are worked on the right side (RS).

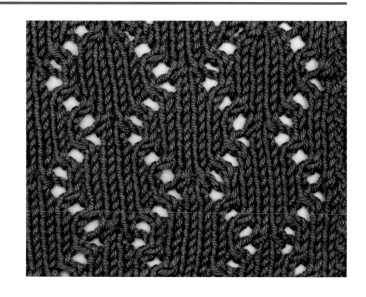

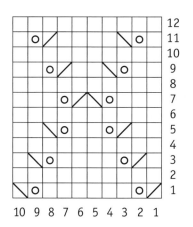

Key

☐ **K:** Knit

◫ **K2tog:** Knit 2 stitches together

◉ **Yo:** Yarn over

◲ **Ssk:** Slip 1 stitch as if to knit, slip another stitch as if to knit, insert the left-hand needle into the front of these 2 stitches and knit them together.

Lace Pattern 3 (12-Stitch Repeat)

Round 1 (RS): P3, yo, k4, k2tog, k3.

Round 2: P3, k1, yo, k4, k2tog, k2.

Round 3: P3, k2, yo, k4, k2tog, k1.

Round 4: P3, k3, yo, k4, k2tog.

Repeat rounds 1–4 for Lace Pattern 3.

NOTE: These instructions assume you are working in the round. All rounds are worked on the right side (RS).

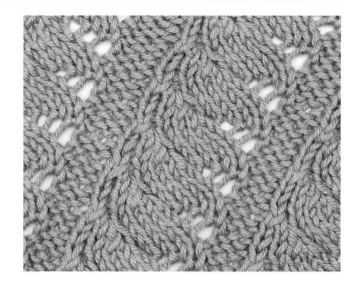

Key

☐ **K:** Knit

● **P:** Purl

○ **Yo:** Yarn over

◢ **K2tog:** Knit 2 stitches together

Lace Pattern 4 (8-Stitch Repeat)

Round 1 (RS): K2, yo, ssk, k1, k2tog, yo, k1.

Round 2: K8.

Round 3: K1, yo, ssk, yo, cdd, yo, k2tog, yo.

Round 4: K8.

Round 5: K1, yo, cdd, yo, k1, yo, cdd, yo.

Round 6: K8.

Round 7: K1, yo, cdd, yo, k1, yo, cdd, yo.

Round 8: K8.

Repeat rounds 1–8 for Lace Pattern 4.

NOTE: These instructions assume you are working in the round. All rounds are worked on the right side (RS).

Key

- ☐ **K:** Knit.

- ⊙ **Yo:** Yarn over.

- ◼ **Ssk:** Slip 1 stitch as if to knit, slip another stich as if to knit, insert the left-hand needle into the front of these 2 stitches and knit them together.

- ◢ **K2tog:** Knit 2 stitches together.

- ⧊ **Cdd (central double decrease):** Slip 2 stiches together as if to knit, k1, pass the 2 slipped stitches over the knit stitch.

Lace Pattern 5 (12-Stitch Repeat)

Round 1 (RS): K1, yo, ssk, yo, k2, cdd, k2, yo, k2tog, yo.

Round 2: K12.

Round 3: K2, yo, ssk, yo, k1, cdd, k1, yo, k2tog, yo, k1.

Round 4: K12.

Round 5: K3, yo, ssk, yo, cdd, yo, k2tog, yo, k2.

Round 6: K12.

Round 7: K1, ssk, yo, k1, yo, ssk, k1, k2tog, yo, k1, yo, k2tog.

Round 8: K12.

Round 9: Cdd, yo, k3, yo, cdd, yo, k3, yo.

Round 10: K12.

Repeat rounds 1–10 for Lace Pattern 5.

NOTE: These instructions assume you are working in the round. All rounds are worked on the right side (RS).

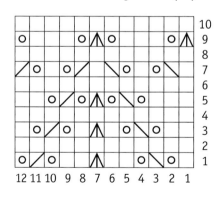

Key

⬜ **K:** Knit.

⊡ **Yo:** Yarn over.

◻ **Ssk:** Slip 1 stitch as if to knit, slip another stich as if to knit, insert the left-hand needle into the front of these 2 stitches and knit them together.

⋀ **Cdd (central double decrease):** Slip 2 stiches together as if to knit, k1, pass the 2 slipped stitches over the knit stitch.

◻ **K2tog:** Knit 2 stitches together.

Lace Pattern 6 (13-Stitch Repeat)

Round 1 (RS): K6, yo, ssk, k5.

Round 2: K13.

Round 3: K4, k2tog, yo, k1, yo, ssk, k4.

Round 4: K13.

Round 5: K3, k2tog, yo, k3, yo, ssk, k3.

Round 6: K13.

Round 7: K2, k2tog, yo, k2, nupp, k2, yo, ssk, k2.

Round 8: K13.

Round 9: K1, k2tog, yo, k1, nupp, k3, nupp, k1, yo, ssk, k1.

Round 10: K13.

Round 11: K2tog, yo, k4, nupp, k4, yo, ssk.

Round 12: K13.

Repeat rounds 1–12 for Lace Pattern 6.

NOTE: These instructions assume you are working in the round. All rounds are worked on the right side (RS).

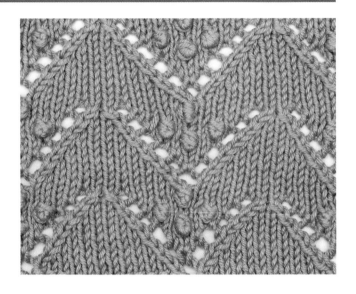

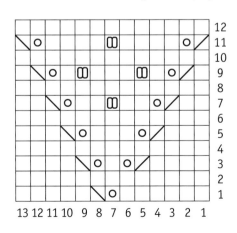

Key

☐ **K:** Knit.

⊙ **Yo:** Yarn over.

◥ **Ssk:** Slip 1 stitch as if to knit, slip another stitch as if to knit, insert the left-hand needle into the front of these 2 stitches and knit them together.

◢ **K2tog:** Knit 2 stitches together.

▥ **Nupp:** (k1, p1, k1, p1, k1) in 1 stitch, pass the first 4 stitches created over the last stitch.

Colorwork patterns are an excellent way to liven up hand-knit items by incorporating a wider range of color into your projects. Although the charts here are presented in hues that match the samples beside them, feel free to experiment with different color combinations. However, be sure to make a swatch with your intended colors before combining them in a larger project. Sometimes things that look good side by side in a skein will not translate well into a full project. There are no line-by-line text directions for the colorwork patterns below because colorwork patterns are usually worked entirely from charted designs.

COLORWORK PATTERN 1

COLORWORK PATTERN 2

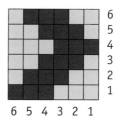

COLORWORK PATTERN 3

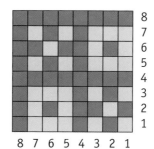

COLORWORK PATTERN 4

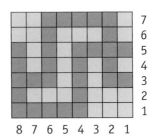

COLORWORK PATTERN 5

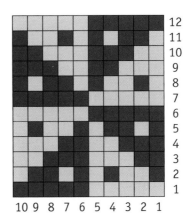

COLORWORK PATTERN 6

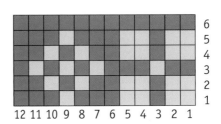

Reference Materials

Decreases

KNIT TWO TOGETHER (K2TOG)

With the yarn at the back of the work, insert the right-hand needle into the next two stitches on the left-hand needle as if to knit, and knit them together.

PURL TWO TOGETHER (P2TOG)

With the yarn at the front of the work, insert the right-hand needle into the next two stitches on the left-hand needle as if to purl and purl them together.

SLIP, SLIP, KNIT (SSK)

With the yarn at the back of the work, slip two stitches, one at a time, as if to knit from the left-hand needle to the right-hand needle. Insert the left-hand needle into the two slipped stitches from left to right, and knit them together

Increases

BACKWARD-LOOP MAKE 1 (MAKE 1)

Using the working yarn, make a backward loop and place it on the right-hand needle so that the working yarn points toward you.

YARN OVER (YO)

Bring the yarn to the front between the two needles. Take the yarn over the right-hand needle to the back so that it is in position to make your next stitch.

Cast-Ons

BACKWARD-LOOP CAST-ON

1 Make a slip knot about 8 inches from the end of the yarn and place it on one of your needles. This counts as your first cast-on stitch.

2 Hold the needle horizontally in your right hand with the tip of the needle pointing to the left. Place your right index finger on top of the loop on the needle to hold the yarn in place. Two strands of yarn will be hanging down from the slip knot: the working yarn (attached to the ball) and the yarn tail (which will be woven in later).

3 Grasp the working yarn with your left hand and position your left thumb horizontally behind this strand.

4 Keeping hold of the working yarn, move your left thumb forward and up so that the yarn wraps around it in a loop. Move the tip of the needle in front of this loop and then into the loop from below.

4

5 Slide the loop onto your needle and off of your thumb. Pull down on the working yarn to gently tighten the loop on the needle.

6 Repeat steps 3–5 until you have cast on the desired number of stitches for your project.

5

FIGURE-EIGHT CAST-ON

1 Hold two short circular needles or the ends of one long circular needle horizontally in your left hand. Arrange them so that one needle is above the other, with the needle tips pointing to the right. Place the yarn between the needles with the about 8 inches of the yarn tail sticking out to the front (toward you). With the thumb of your left hand, hold the yarn tail against the front of the bottom needle.

2 With your right hand, wrap the working yarn up over the top needle, to the front, and then back between the needles.

2

3 Next, wrap the working yarn down under the bottom needle, to the front, and then back between the needles.

4 Repeat steps 2–3 until you have cast on the correct number of stitches for your project, checking that you have the same number of stitches on the top and bottom needles. The stitches on the top needle will be worked first as side 1 of the project; the stitches on the bottom needle will be worked next as side 2.

NOTE: Due to the way that this cast on wraps the yarn around the needles, you must work the stitches on side 2 through the back loop to prevent them from being twisted.

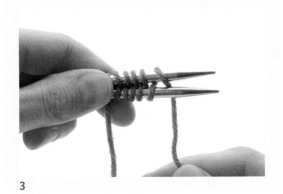

3

LONG-TAIL CAST-ON
See page 28.

Bind-Offs

BASIC BIND-OFF
See page 65.

THREE-NEEDLE BIND-OFF

1 Arrange your work so that each set of stitches to be bound off is on a separate needle. Hold these needles in your left hand, with the right sides of the work together, the needles parallel, and the needle points to the right.

1

2 Using a third needle, knit the first stitch on the front needle and the first stitch on the back needle together and slide them off of the left-hand needles.

3 Work Step 2 again so that two stitches are now on the right-hand needle.

2

4 With one of the left-hand needles, lift the first knit stitch on the right-hand needle over the second and off the needle (as for the basic bind-off).

5 Repeat steps 3-4 until all the stitches have been bound off and only one loop remains on the right-hand needle.

6 Cut the yarn, leaving an 8-inch tail. Slip the final loop off the needle and pull this loop up until the yarn tail comes free and the loop no longer remains.

4

Seaming

KITCHENER STITCH

1. Arrange your stitches on two needles with an equal number on each needle. Cut the working yarn leaving a tail three times as long as the intended finished edge. Thread this tail onto a seaming needle.

2. Hold both needles horizontally in your left hand, with the tips of the needles pointing to the right. The needle with the last worked stitch should be to the back. Hold the seaming needle in your right hand.

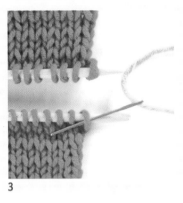

3

3. Bring the seaming needle through the first stitch on the **front** needle as if to **purl**, pulling the yarn through the stitch while leaving the stitch on the needle.

4. Bring the seaming needle through the first stitch on the **back** needle as if to **knit**, pulling the yarn through the stitch while leaving the stitch on the needle.

4

5. Bring the seaming needle through the first stitch on the **front** needle as if to **knit** (a), pull the yarn through the stitch, and slide the stitch **off** the needle (b).

a

b

6 Bring the seaming needle through the next stitch on the **front** needle as if to **purl,** and leave it on the needle.

7 Bring the seaming needle through the first stitch on the **back** needle as if to **purl** (a) and slide it **off** the needle. Then bring the seaming needle through the next stitch on the **back** needle as if to **knit** (b) and leave it on the needle.

8 Repeat steps 5–7 until one stitch remains on each needle.

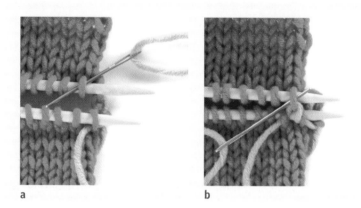

a   b

9 Finish by passing the seaming needle through the front stitch as if to knit and sliding it off the needle, then passing the needle through the back stitch as if to purl and sliding it off the needle. Bring the yarn tail to the inside of the work and weave in the end.

WHIPSTITCH

1 Cut a piece of yarn that is three times the width of the intended seam and thread it onto a seaming needle.

2 With the right sides of the work facing one another, pull the needle through both pieces in the upper right corner from back to front leaving a 8-inch tail.

3 Take the needle up and over the work to the back and pull the needle through both pieces from back to front about ¼ of an inch from the last stitch. Pull gently to snug up the stitch. Repeat across the seam.

4 When the seam is complete, weave in all yarn ends.

3

Other Terms

"AS IF TO KNIT"

When a pattern says "slip the next stitch as if to knit," insert your needle into the next stitch from front to back as if you were going to knit it, then slip it to the right-hand needle without knitting it.

"AS IF TO PURL"

When a pattern says "slip the next stitch as if to purl," insert your needle into the next stitch from back to front as if you were going to purl it, then slip it to the right-hand needle without purling it.

RIGHT SIDE OF THE WORK (RS)

When a pattern specifies the "right side" of the work, this means the side of the work that faces the public when the project is completed. It is most often the knit side of stockinette stitch, but this will vary depending on the stitch pattern used.

WRONG SIDE OF THE WORK (WS)

When a pattern specifies the "wrong side" of the work, this means the inside of the work when the project is completed. It is most often the purl side of stockinette stitch, but this will vary depending on the stitch pattern used.

Resources

Berroco, Inc.
14 Elmdale Road
P.O. Box 367
Uxbridge, MA 01569
www.berroco.com

Blue Moon Fiber Arts Inc.
56587 Mollenhour Road
Scappoose, OR 97056
www.bluemoonfiberarts.com

Buffalo Gold
www.buffalogold.net

Clover-USA
Chibi tapestry needles, locking stitch markers
13438 Alondra Boulevard
Cerritos, CA 90703
www.clover-usa.com

DyakCraft
P.O. Box 721
Saxtons River, VT 05154
www.dyakcraft.com

Foxfire Fiber and Design
135 Reynolds Road
Shelburne, MA 01370
www.foxfirefiber.com

Lion Brand Yarn
135 Kero Road
Carlstadt, NJ 07072
www.lionbrand.com

Lorna's Laces
4229 North Honore Street
Chicago, IL 60613
www.lornaslaces.net

Peace Fleece
475 Porterfield Road
Porter, ME 04068
www.peacefleece.com

Schaefer Yarn Company
3514 Kelly's Corners Road
Interlaken, NY 14847
www.schaeferyarn.com

Skacel Collection, Inc.
Addi Natura, Turbo, and Lace needles
P.O. Box 88110
Seattle, WA 98138
www.skacelknitting.com

Signature Needle Arts
signatureneedlearts.com

Spirit Trail Fiberworks
P.O. Box 197
Sperryville, VA 22740-0197
www.spirit-trail.net

Valley Fibers/WEBS
75 Service Center Drive
Northampton, MA 01060
www.yarn.com

Stitched by JessaLu
Jessica L. Meyer
jessalu@gmail.com
www.stitchedbyjessalu.com
413-591-8496

Index

Yearning to do more with yarn?

Packed with photos, patterns, and step-by-step instructions, you'll love knitting the visual way!

978-0-470-27896-3   978-0-470-07782-5   978-0-470-06817-5

WILEY
Now you know.